RONALD KNOX was born in 1888, the son of the Anglican Bishop of Manchester. He became a convert to the Catholic Church in 1917 and subsequently served as chaplain to the Catholic students at Oxford University. He gave this up in order to devote his full time to the translation of the Bible into contemporary English, a monumental job he completed in nine years. Msgr. Knox died in 1957. He wrote a great variety of books, including scriptural commentaries, satire, detective stories and sermons.

THE MASS IN SLOW MOTION

THE MASS IN SLOW MOTION

By
RONALD KNOX

NEW YORK
SHEED & WARD

COPYRIGHT, 1948, BY SHEED & WARD, INC.

BX
2230
K5

NIHIL OBSTAT: E. C. MESSENGER, Ph.D.
CENSOR DEPUTATUS

IMPRIMATUR: E. MORROGH BERNARD
VIC. GEN.

WESTMONASTERII, DIE 24A MAII, 1948

This book is copyright. No portion of it may be reproduced without written permission. Inquiries should be addressed to the publishers.

PRINTED
IN THE UNITED STATES OF AMERICA

To Nicola . . .

PREFACE

IF I HAVE a public, this book, I fear, will be a severe test of its patience. That a priest should put on record his private thoughts about the Mass—there is nothing extravagant in that. But mine were put on record in a highly specialized art-form, that of sermons to school-girls; and this form they still impenitently wear. There are films which a child can frequent only by pretending to be an adult. Here are pages which an adult can enjoy only by pretending to be a child. *Nisi efficiamini sicut parvuli* . . .

The sermons were preached to the convent school of the Assumption Sisters, which was "evacuated" during the late war from Kensington to Aldenham Park in Shropshire. They appeared afterwards in *The Tablet*, much abridged; by reducing them to less than half their original size, it was possible to give them the air of a contribution designed for that paper. They are now offered to the public almost in their original form. The few excisions which have been made were made reluctantly; no word I had written but recalled some memory not lightly exorcised, and I will not pretend to have finished the business of proof-reading altogether dry-eyed.

Only the introductory sermon (though this, too, was preached at Aldenham) was written for grown-ups. It is included here to give a preview of the whole subject; a breathless introduction to a slow-motion picture. If you want to dip into the book, you need go no further. If you read it, and find yourself wanting to remember what it said, this first chapter will suffice to refresh your memory.

But this book must not be published without a special greeting to the Sisters of the Assumption, and some pupils of theirs who are school-girls no longer. These, with memories for their book-markers, will be (I hope) the indulgent critics they always were; even utility sermons grow easier with custom.

R. A. KNOX.

MELLS,
Easter, 1948.

INTRODUCTION

SOMEBODY, I forget who, wrote his reminiscences of the years 1914–18 under the title, *One Man's War*. I thought I should like to plagiarize that title and make up a kind of meditation under the heading, *One Priest's Mass*. I suppose it is the experience of all of us that the Mass, with its terrific uniformity—unvarying throughout Latin Christendom, varying so little from one feast or season to another—does not impose uniformity on our thoughts. Merely because the words and gestures are so familiar, we don't rest content with their immediate significance; we read fresh meanings of our own into them, treat them as a kind of cipher language in which we communicate our aspirations to Almighty God. It's an odd reflection, then, that when I say Mass or you hear it, though the words and the gestures are the same, and you would think there was no difference at all except the sins we thought about at the *Confiteor* and the intentions we remembered for the living and the dead, *in fact* there is a difference; the devotional overtones, the mystical nuances which the words and the ceremonies of the Mass suggest to us are not, probably, the same for you and for me. So I thought I would come clean, and try to analyse, thus publicly, the inwardness of my own Mass; talk about the odd bells that ring in my own mind, the odd vistas that open up to my own view, to close again at once, in the hope that they may have some value for other people. Let me say at once that I know nothing about liturgy, so you won't get any of the orthodox side-lights on the Mass which they give you in the books. Also that I am thinking about Low Mass; it is a long time since I had to sing High Mass, and when I did, the only thought I can remember entertaining was a vivid hope that I might die before we got to the Preface.

The Psalm *Judica*. What a disconcerting thing it is about the idiom of Hebrew devotion, that the psalms are always saying, "I am upright, I am innocent, I never did anything to deserve this punishment", whereas we are always wanting to say we are miserable sinners! Here, we prepare for the *Confiteor* by assuring God that we have walked innocently, and asking him to distinguish very carefully between us and the wicked. When I say this psalm, then, what should I think about? Perhaps, about myself as the representative of the Christian Church, so isolated, so shut away, in idea at least, from all the busy wickedness of the world. The Mass starts with the Church pushing the world away from her; the lodge is tiled, there are no profane onlookers, it is a cosy family party, just ourselves.

Then the *Confiteor*; that is more personal. Not that, I fancy, we are meant to be thinking precisely about our sins, rather about our sinfulness; not so much the sinners we are as the sinful sort of people we are; with no right to claim the sort of intimacy we are going to claim in coming before God. Well, we shall have to remember that God is Almighty and merciful, and go ahead as best we can. And then that splendid ceremony of kissing the altar as you say *Quorum reliquiae hic sunt*. A keyhole through which you look right back to the catacombs; Mass over the tombs of the martyrs; the Church unageing, her days bound each to each by natural piety.

The Introit gives you a nice sense of squaring your shoulders and opening out a bit; you have forgotten the fears and scruples that assailed you at the foot of the altar; you crash into the liturgy of the day in a good hearty voice. And then suddenly the old trouble comes back again, only I think in a different form. Sins or no sins, what are you, a man, a creature, that you should be standing up and talking to God like this, as if a conversation with him were the most natural thing in the world? Back you go to the middle of the altar, feeling an utter worm; *Kyrie eleison*, again and again, begging his pardon for your ridiculous self-sufficiency in imagining, even for a moment, that you had a right to stand up straight, instead of burying your head in your hands. You remind yourself, with the *Gloria*, of what God is, in a stammering, apologetic sort of way, so that you find yourself thanking him for being so glorious—not a thing you do as a rule. And from that you turn to a paean of praise in honour of our Blessed Lord, hiding behind him, covering yourself in him, to get the technique of your approach to Almighty God right after all. And so you go back to your post at the side, a little reassured, and start again with the Collects.

I rather like a lot of Collects. It's nice to have a lot of different subjects of conversation when you are going to talk to God. When people ask us to say a prayer for some particular intention, our first reaction is perhaps to think it a nuisance. But surely we ought to regard each intention as a new excuse for claiming God's attention, like a child that thinks it fun to be sent on a message to its father, because it is so splendid to be allowed, for once, to interrupt him in his study. So with these obscurer saints, these much-thumbed imperatas; an excellent opportunity for making our conversation with God last longer. The Collects we ought to think of perhaps as SOS messages expressing, in as brief terms as possible, the needs of the Church. Then, for the Epistle, there is a relaxing of strain. The Epistle is a letter, written quite a long time ago, to us; and we read it out in a leisurely way. For once—it is the only part of the Mass of which you can say that—you stand at ease. Your hands escape from their rigid discipline. It is an interval, a pause; accidentally protracted by one or two bits of liturgy which were so obviously meant to be sung that they do not go naturally at Low Mass. Even the Sequences, beautiful as they are, seem to cry out for the music; they are not reciting pieces.

And now you have an expedition to make; a sort of Polar expedition to the unvisited wilds at the north end of the altar. Nothing is ever said or done there, except for the reading out of the words of life, extracts from those precious fragments which tell us what happened when God came to earth. Accordingly, we brace ourselves for this unaccustomed journey by a special dedication of our lips, those unclean lips of ours which are responsible, all day long, for so much gossip, uncharity, unkindness, grousing, flattery, boasting, and perhaps even profanity; they need a kind of salve before we take the words of life on them. And not only our lips, you will notice, but our hearts.

That's the tragedy of it, that the Gospel never seems to grip us . . . you see, we know it by heart. What an odd phrase that is, isn't it, " knowing a thing by heart ". Because, when we are talking about the Gospels, that's just the way we don't know them. Still, one reads the Gospel, and kisses the book at the end, and hopes that somehow the message of it will steal through those lips into the heart which has read through it so coldly, so inattentively.

Then, if it is one of those big days, you get the *Credo* as something of a relief; if charity has burnt so low, there is still faith anyhow; the *Credo*, with those phrases at the beginning which send your mind, sometimes, rocketing up heavenwards without very much consciousness of what it is you are saying; and the splendid dramatic moment of *Et homo factus est*, with the noise of kicking and scraping behind you, where rheumatic knees are being laboriously bent in honour of God made Man. And then follows the odd *Dominus vobiscum* and *Oremus* which isn't followed by a prayer; I suppose it once came just in front of the Secret prayers, or something like that. Standing inconclusive as it does, it has the suggestion of being a mere excuse for taking a peep behind you, and seeing that the congregation are still there. Good, they are. This is where the congregation get their look in. The Offertory is, in theory, the whole congregation surging up into the sanctuary and presenting you, the priest, with the bread and wine, their contribution to the mysteries.

Actually, in their name, a small boy emerges from the background, probably with hiccoughs; at first sight you are tempted to regard him as an unwelcome distraction, then you remember that he stands there in the name of the congregation, offering you unconsecrated wine, and saying, "I suppose this wouldn't be any use?" Then the *Lavabo*, with the psalm in which you start protesting your own innocence, just as at the *Praeparatio*. Once more, the lodge is being tiled; the catechumens are supposed to be going away; once more we remind ourselves that we are a family party. The Secret prayers are said over the unconsecrated bread and wine, and are always about them. It is as if we had to whisper them in our embarrassment, feeling, like the boy with the five loaves again, how ridiculously inadequate they are as the raw material for a miracle; just as everything we give to God is ridiculously inadequate to the purposes for which his grace makes it effective. You will often find that apologetic note in the Secret prayers.

Then comes the first of those three sudden emergences from silence into sound, with the words *Per omnia saecula saeculorum*, that lend to the Mass, from the unliturgical layman's point of view, a good deal of its atmosphere of mystery. When you hear it from the congregation, you feel as if the priest was being torn between two different instincts; one of which tells him that what he is saying is much too sacred to be said out loud, while the other tells him that it is much too important *not* to be said out loud—first one instinct, then the other, getting the mastery. From the priest's own point of view, I think this first *Per omnia* has an evident psychological value. The mind tends to accompany the voice, by force of habit; and the mere fact of breaking out into speech after a happily-arranged preface of silence encourages the mind to an outburst of praise, just at a moment when it is apt to have gone off day-dreaming. And I think it has a symbolic value in that way. We ought, obviously, to be praising God at every moment of our lives. Obviously we aren't. Consequently, when we do start praising God it is right that we should do it in a sort of nervous scurry, like a man who has just remembered that he has got a train to catch. The *Sursum corda* which invites us to praise incites us, at the same time, to contrition; how terrible that our hearts should be continually grovelling, and have to be hoisted up in this almost undignified way on the rare occasions when we really do praise God!

And then the splendours of the Preface, with the various ranks of Angels flashing past us like the names of suburban stations as we draw closer to the heart of a great capital. The holy Angels, I think, have a knack of drawing up one's mind to God, by being at once so awe-inspiring and at the same time so obviously inconclusive; the attitude of the Angel in the Apocalypse, who will not let St. John worship him and bids him worship God instead, is permanently their attitude. And at the same time, the glimpse we catch of those Angels who veil their faces before the throne warns us that the loud, confident tone in which we cried *Sursum corda* must be modified a little as we reach the threshold; that slight drop of the voice for the *Sanctus* just chastens our praises with a salutary touch of awe.

On that threshold, we pause a little, to remind ourselves that we are not alone. In case we were in danger—the younger of us, anyhow, fresh from the splendour of ordination—of feeling self-important about the tremendous office we hold, the tremendous business we are transacting, we reflect that the man who stands here is only *a* priest of the universal Church; at the moment when he consecrates, he is the particular unit in whom her prayer is being manifested. He is the particular sentry who happens to be posted at this particular spot, under orders from his Bishop. He must think of himself as an inconsiderable unit of this great army whose whole cause now, all the multitudinous needs of the Church of God, he proceeds to recommend to God: then, and not till then, he may make his private *Memento.* A sudden close-up; for a moment, the features of one particular individual, or one particular situation, disentangle themselves from the general muddle God's world is in, and stand out clearly before your mind; there, that is enough, we shall not add to the value of the Mass by interrupting it with our wool-gatherings. . . . Our intention is not the only intention; each of the worshippers behind us has a private one; *et omnium circumstantium,* take just as much notice, Lord, of theirs as of mine. But, after all, we are all *communicantes,* we are all parts of this tremendous whole, the Church; and we all share the intercessions of the saints, who are the Church's property. " Whether Paul, or Cephas, all are yours "; then the familiar string of names; Italians, most of them, what does it matter? All are yours; and you are Christ's, and Christ is God's; let us get on with the Mass.

You hurry on to the Consecration, after a few more last-moment gestures, as if to make the still unconsecrated elements less unworthy of what they are going to become. And then, with the Consecration itself, you go off on to a quite different tack. You stop making up prayers, thinking up reverential epithets, piling strings of participles together; you don't ask God for anything or apologize for anything or try to induce any attitude or any frame of mind in yourself; you simply stand there and record a piece of history. In recording that piece of history, it becomes necessary to recite some words our Lord used; and so, as if absent-mindedly, almost as if unintentionally, you do what you came there to do; or rather, you don't do it, you suddenly pull yourself together and realize that our Lord's words, even relaid on such lips as yours, have done it. A moment ago, you could move your hands quite freely; now, an extraordinary sort of paralysis has fallen on them, so that it is impossible to separate the thumbs from the index fingers. Christ has used you to do a miracle, and everything has become quite different. You elevate the Host, the Chalice; or are they trying to fly upwards out of your hands? You hardly know, it is all so strange.

Anyhow, you start offering this precious Thing that has fallen between your hands; you connect it with this and that, the mysteries of our Lord's life, the Old Testament sacrifices, the ministry of the Angels in Heaven, the expectation of the faithful dead; another string of saints' names occurs to you; but all this you do in a half-dazed way, still thinking about what it is that lies before you; and then, boldly, you take up Host and Chalice together and hold them up for a breathless moment. And then suddenly you are talking out loud again, and feel the ground sure under your feet as you find yourself saying the *Pater Noster.* I suppose each of us has a clause or a phase of the Mass at which, if it wasn't for the trouble and confusion it was going to cause, he would like to die. Mine is the *Pater Noster*. It is, to me, the moment in the Mass at which one is most consciously, most fearlessly, talking to God.

Almost immediately afterwards, at the end of the *Libera nos*, we start doing something we haven't yet done in the Mass since we said the *Gloria*, except perhaps momentarily in a Collect; we start talking to Jesus Christ. The sacrifice is over, the banquet has begun; and we do what we can to reconcile ourselves to the bewildering fact of his condescension to our needs. *A te numquam separari permittas*—that is the kernel of it; when that is said, all is said. So the priest gives you Communion. If the priest is yourself, you are hardly conscious of that. You are receiving, not giving. As for the Communion of the Faithful—at least if there are many—how difficult it is not to feel this as an interruption in " my Mass! " But of course there is no such thing as " my Mass "; we are ministers before we are priests, and it is for us to wait (hours, if need be) on our ministering.

And so the Mass comes to an end, in a whirl of purifications and postscripts, that do not seek to impress themselves deeply on the mind; one has not enough capacity left for receiving impressions. There is a tag which occurs frequently in the Old Testament, and once in the New, " And every man went to his own house "; that is what we do at the *Ite missa est*; the coming of Christ to our souls is a thing too intimate for liturgy; we must be alone. As the priest gives the Blessing and says the last Gospel, he is only (as it were) covering his retreat; we know it is all over, really.

So much of drama, every day of our lives; and we, how little we are thrilled by it!

CONTENTS

I

AT THE FOOT OF THE ALTAR

I will go up to the altar of God, the giver of youth and happiness. Ps. xlii.

I

AT THE FOOT OF THE ALTAR

I will go up to the altar of God, the giver of youth and happiness. Ps. xlii.

SOME time last spring, I think it was, I gave you a sermon[1] about what it felt like saying Mass. I shall now go on to expand that into about twelve different ones, taking the various parts of the Mass as they come. Not merely the words; the Mass is actions as well as words, in fact the whole time it is suiting the actions to the words. Monsignor Robert Hugh Benson, years ago, wrote rather an interesting thing—you will find it in his *Papers of a Pariah*—in which he suggested that the Mass is really a kind of religious dance, a symbolic dance. Of course that sounds nonsense to you, because what you mean by a dance is the wireless in the hall playing revolting stuff and you lounging round in pairs and feeling all gooey. But dancing when it first started meant something, and nearly always something religious. So Hugh Benson's idea was that the Christian faith has a religious dance of its own; all the twisting and turning, and bobbing and bowing, and lifting and parting and rejoining his hands, which the priest goes through in the course of the Mass, really add up to a kind of dance, meant to express a religious idea to you, the spectators.

[1] Included in the introductory sermon in this book.

Of course, as I'm always telling you, if you find it difficult or if you find it dull trying to follow the Mass, you are much better employed in simply kneeling there and saying your prayers, with a book or without a book, *while Mass is going on.* The Church doesn't oblige you to follow Mass; she only obliges you, now and again, to be there. But if you are going to try and follow the Mass, it's a good thing to try and understand what the words are ABOUT, not just get accustomed to them as a kind of pious rigmarole; and it's a good thing to see the gestures which the priest makes as the proper accompaniment of those words, illustrating and expressing them, instead of vaguely imagining that he is waving his arms about for no particular reason.

Well, this afternoon we'll just take the part which the priest says at the foot of the altar, which is quite enough for one go. I don't know if you have ever wondered why the remark which the priest makes at the very start is "I will go unto the altar of God" when he is there already. The explanation of that is that originally the Mass began with the Introit (that's what the priest says a few moments later, at the Epistle side of the altar), and ended with the *Ite missa est*; the rest is really trimmings. This psalm and the *Confiteor* the priest used originally to say in the sacristy; it's only since Pius V's time that it has really been part of the Mass. If we were living in the time of King Henry VIII, I should be saying the psalm and the *Confiteor* while you were looking for your berets. But don't, for that reason, think that this first part of the Mass doesn't matter, and it's a good opportunity for having a look round to see that the lay sisters are all there. It's part of the Mass, now. And all the Mass belongs to you, and you to it, if you are really going to follow it. The action of the Mass is polarized, is focused in the priest, that's all. Those are rather long words; let me explain a bit. If you have a burning-glass, and are concentrating its rays on a single point, a bit of touchwood, to make the touchwood light, or the back of another girl's hand, to make her jump, the light comes to a point, and that red-hot point is the priest; but all the part in between the burning-glass and that red-hot point is comfortably warm—that is you, the congregation. You are meant to be basking in that heat which ought to be making the priest, the focus-point of it all, melt away with love. So start straight away, with the priest; square your shoulders with him and cross yourself, thinking to yourself " In the name of the Father, and of the Son, and of the Holy Ghost "; here we are, let's get on with it.

What is this psalm the priest says? Unfortunately, we don't know much for certain about the psalms and the occasions on which they were first written. Some people think this one was written by King David when he fled from Absalom. I don't know if you all know that story; but Absalom was a son of King David's who revolted against him and got made king instead, and then there was a battle in which David's men got the better of the revolutionaries; but whether he really wrote this psalm I don't know. It talks about " the God who gives me the gladness of youth "; King David at the time of Absalom's revolt was getting on for sixty, and you don't feel much joy of youth when you are getting on for sixty. So some people think that the author of the psalm, or at any rate the imaginary hero of the psalm, was a young priest or a young Levite exiled from his native country, we don't know when or why, who was simply longing to get his sentence of exile reversed, and get back to the Temple and the altar of God, where he had been so happy. Now let us just go through the psalm; I'll give it you, if you don't mind, in my own translation.

" O God, sustain my cause; give me redress against a race that knows no piety; save me from a treacherous foe and cruel. Thou, O God, art all my strength, why hast thou cast me off? Why do I go mourning, with enemies pressing me hard? The light of thy favour, the fulfilment of thy promise, let these be my escort, bringing me safe to thy holy mountain, to the tabernacle where thou dwellest. There I will go up to the altar of God, the giver of youth and happiness; thou art my God, with the harp I will hymn thy praise. Soul, why art thou downcast, why art thou all lament? Wait for God's help; I will not cease to cry out in thankfulness, my champion and my God."

I've used that word " champion ", rather spoiled by the way in which we use it nowadays, to express what I think the psalm means when it says, " the saviour of my face ". The man who saves your face, the man who makes it possible for you to appear in public without looking a fool. I think our hero is labouring somehow under unjust suspicion, cast upon him by his enemies, and so he wants God to sustain his cause, establish his innocence; to save his face, to make it possible for him to reappear at Jerusalem, and in the Temple, without a stain on his character. And that is partly why it is such a good psalm to begin the Mass with; because inevitably the priest feels rather a fool having to stand up there and look good, when he is really a sinful man like his fellow men; and he wants a champion to come and keep him in countenance, keep him in face, as we say. . . . I wonder whether all that comes home to you? It depends on whether you are shy; some of you are, some aren't. If you are at all shy, you can imagine how appalling it would be if your mamma told you quite suddenly one morning that you were going to be presented at Court. If she went on to say that unfortunately there was no time to get any special clothes, and you would have to go just as you were, that would put the lid on your misery, wouldn't it? And that is how a priest feels or ought to feel when he goes to the altar. He is presenting himself at the Court of Heaven, before the throne of the King of Kings, among crowds and crowds of angels and saints, and he is all just anyhow, quite unfit for such company. He can't face the prospect at all unless our Blessed Lord will be kind enough to take him by the hand and lead him in and say, " This is a friend of mine ". That is why he says the psalm *Judica me Deus*.

And you ought to be keeping step with the priest in this first movement, as it were, of the religious dance. The priest is standing there with his arms in front of him staring up at the crucifix over the altar; an attitude of appeal. And that ought to be the attitude of your mind to start with; you oughtn't ever to go to Mass, and still more obviously you oughtn't ever to go to Communion, without this sense of shyness, this sense of butting in somewhere where you aren't wanted. We're terribly in danger all the time of taking God's goodness too much for granted; of bouncing up to Communion as if it were the most natural thing in the world, instead of being a supernatural thing belonging to another world. So first we must be shy about it; then we must observe that the priest's attitude, though it is one of appeal, is also one of confident appeal. " Soul, why art thou downcast? " he says, " Why art thou all lament? " And the server chimes in " Wait for God's help "—it's all right really, he will see us through; he is our champion, will stand at our side and make everything all right for us. So it is that the priest, at the end of the psalm, says, " I *will* go up to the altar of God, after all "; crosses himself, to give him extra courage, and reminds himself, " Our help is in the name of the Lord, who made heaven and earth ". Yes, it's all right, he will see us through.

But meanwhile you look up and find that there has been a sudden change in the movement of the dance. The priest, who was standing so erect, is all doubled up now. It is the *Confiteor*. Catching sight of himself out of the corner of his eye standing up there and telling himself he is sure our Lord will make it all right, he gets a kind of sudden scruple—his sins! Even sins committed since he last said Mass, right in the foreground of memory; the man who lost his temper so idiotically only yesterday, the man who only yesterday said that unkind thing, calculated to hurt and meant to hurt the person he was talking to—what right has he to expect any divine favours, to ask that he may have God's light and God's truth for his escort, to lead him up to the altar? So he grovels, accuses himself of his sins in the sight of Heaven. And not only in the sight of Heaven, in the sight of earth too. Every sin you or I commit is letting down the whole Christian community, isn't it? Just as you apologize to your partner when you've made a perfectly rotten stroke at tennis, so when you have sinned you want to apologize to your fellow-Christians; you have let them all down. And then there is that splendid bit of spiritual by-play, the priest asking the servers to pray for him, and the servers turning round to explain that they are just as bad. It's a sort of open confession all round. When there are priests in choir, you know, they are supposed to mumble all this part of the Mass to one another while the priest is getting through it at the altar. We are all making a clean breast of it, putting our cards on the table.

That means that if you are trying to follow the Mass you mustn't regard the *Confiteor* as a private affair of the priest's, and imagine it would be more tactful of you to pretend not to notice. You mustn't listen to the server's mumbled apologies in a spirit of detachment. No, it is *your* sins that he is confessing, quite as much as his own. Or rather perhaps not so much your sins as your *sinfulness*; it isn't so much this and that spiteful or greedy or careless action we ought to be remembering at this point in the Mass, rather the general low level of spirituality in us which is *always* making us do spiteful or greedy or careless things. We're a rotten crowd, all of us, that's the point. And when the priest beats his breast three times, or when the server does it, you ought to be echoing the sentiment; we are doing a grovel all round.

And now the priest strikes a fresh attitude, a fresh figure in the dance; he is no longer bent double, but he is bowing slightly, as he says the remaining four versicles before going up to the altar. He is tantalizing himself, as it were, by not looking up to the Cross, not looking up to the altar, just yet; that is a treat he is saving up for himself. Yes, my God, you will put life into us, dead things as we are, and we, this whole *plebs*, this whole vulgar crowd of people, will boast of your protection. You will shew us your mercy, your power to aid. You will listen to our prayers; this silly noise we are making will reach you, right up in the courts of Heaven. And then, just to make sure that he is carrying the congregation with him, he says, "The Lord be with you". And the server answers, "And with you likewise" (that is all "And with thy spirit" means). Priest and people are going about this great business of theirs shoulder to shoulder. Then at last the priest lifts his eyes, and makes that sort of scooping gesture with his hands, as if to gather up any stray strands of grace that may be floating down to him. And he says, "Let us pray". Good idea; let's.

II

INTROIT, KYRIE, GLORIA

Glory to God in high heaven, and peace on earth to the men that are God's friends. Luke ii.

II

INTROIT, KYRIE, GLORIA

Glory to God in high heaven, and peace on earth to the men that are God's friends. Luke ii.

WE LEFT the priest last Sunday at the foot of the altar; he has told us to get busy praying, and now he strides away from us; purposefully, like a man who knows what he is about; rather like our Lord going up to Judaea for his Passion, when the Gospels tell us that "his face was set towards Jerusalem". I think you will find that most priests are walking rather fast, a good deal faster than their usual pace, over those two or three steps. Indeed, if you could see inside the priest's mind, you would almost say he was running up the steps. It reminds me of some lines in a poem none of you know, a poem called "David in Heaven". It says there "His feet trip without a slip, Going to the altar". Well, of course it wouldn't really do to run; it isn't a bit easy to run upstairs in a cassock, and then there is generally lace on the end of one's alb, on purpose so that one shall put one's foot through it if one isn't careful. And besides, the motion of that dance is meant to be slow all through. But the priest is mentally running, so to speak; all through that business with the server which we were talking about last Sunday he has been tantalizing himself, as it were, by not going up just yet; very much as some of you would tantalize yourselves, on receiving a really exciting parcel, by insisting on undoing the knots before you looked inside it. The priest rushes up to the altar and kisses it; he can't hold himself in any longer. He didn't kiss it when he went up before, to arrange the things, because he wasn't really beginning the Mass then. Now he goes up and kisses it. And the meaning of that movement in the dance is obvious, I hope, even to the stupidest of us. It is meant to express the great desire we ought to have for God, the desire to get closer to him, get in contact with him, which is the real reason for our saying any prayers at all.

What he kisses, actually, is the corporal, the big white thing folded in nine squares which he takes out of the large green envelope on the top of the chalice. Underneath the corporal is—what? Three thicknesses of altar-cloth. Underneath the altar-cloths is—what? A piece of stone all wrapped up in waxed cloth, so as to be waterproof. That stone has been consecrated long ago, by a bishop; and the bishop in consecrating it fills up some holes in it with—what do you think? Tiny bits of relics of the saints. People used to use relics of that kind rather freely in the Middle Ages; they used to put them into bridges, for instance, so as to be sure that the bridges held up. I know a very old bridge on the upper Thames where you can still see, in the masonry at the side, a kind of socket where they obviously used to keep the relics of some saint long ago. King Henry the Sixth (no, not King Henry the Eighth; King Henry the Sixth, Wars of the Roses) used to be regarded as a saint before the Reformation, and they kept a relic of his on the bridge between Caversham and Reading, and another relic of his, so I've been told, on the bridge at Bridgnorth. Well, that's all beside the point; nowadays it is only altars that have to have relics in them; but they've jolly well got to. Even a military chaplain carries round with him an altar stone, with relics let into it, and he must never say Mass without having that stone on the soap-box or whatever it is he is using for an altar. And if you ask why the Church should insist on that rather inconvenient regulation, the simplest answer is this; if he didn't, he would start the Mass by telling a lie.

I hope you all remember that the Mass proper hasn't started yet; all that preparation business we were talking about last Sunday was only preparation really. Now, just as he is going to begin the Mass proper, the priest rushes up to the altar, kisses it, and says, " We beseech thee, O Lord, *by the merits of those saints whose relics are here*, and of all the saints, to be indulgent towards my sins ". The saints whose relics are here—why is that so important? Why, because in the very early days, when the Christians at Rome were being persecuted, they used to meet for worship in the catacombs just outside the city. The catacombs are miles and miles of underground passages, which you can still explore with a guide if you go out to Rome. There the Christians used to bury the poor mangled remains of their friends who had been killed in the persecution; and on the tombstones raised over these bodies of the martyrs the Roman bishop used to say Mass. And when the priest, saying those words, kisses the tiny relics tucked away in the altar-stone, he reminds himself, if he has any sense of history, that by that action he is putting himself in touch, so to speak, with the Universal Church that is in Communion with Rome. All altars, all over the world, are one altar really, the mother-altar of Christendom; all altars must have relics in them, so as to remind us that we belong to the martyrs of the first century, and they to us. St. John, in the Apocalypse, says " I saw beneath the altar the souls of all who had been slain for love of God's word "; some people think that is a reference to this habit of saying Mass over the martyrs' tombs—it's as old as that. And when you see the priest kissing the altar just then, you may think of Christian history, all through these nineteen centuries, as linked up. The Mass is all one, in A.D. 48 or in A.D. 1948; the Mass is all one, in the catacombs at Rome or in the tin chapel. That altar-stone is a kind of keyhole through which you get a glimpse into the whole of our Christian past.

However, we mustn't spend all the afternoon talking about one particular moment in the Mass. Now we come to one of the really exciting points, don't we; the point at which you have to *find your place in the missal*, so as to shew the girl next to you that you are pretty well up in these things. I mean, if you take any trouble about it beforehand—I bet you don't—you will have your thumb firmly fixed into your missal at the fourth Sunday after Epiphany before the Mass starts.

What does the priest do? He puts on his spectacles. Up to now, all that he has said is something he says, word for word, every day of his life, except in the black Masses when he leaves out the psalm *Judica*. But now we have reached the point at which the Mass begins to be changeable, the Introit. The Introit I said this morning was that of the fourth Sunday after Epiphany, not the same as St. Winefride's, yesterday, or the Holy Souls on Friday, or All Saints on Thursday. Priests are apt to develop a rather self-satisfied way of saying the Introit, as if to imply, " Now we really are getting down to it ". Do you ever get taken out to lunch at a restaurant by an uncle? And if so, don't you find that he sits down, pulls out his spectacles, and looks through the menu saying or as if to say, " Well, let's see what they are giving us to-day "? Same old spam of course, but that gesture of his survives from the days of plenty. The Introit is a bit like that; it is a foretaste of what the Mass on this particular day is going to be about. In form, it is a short sentence, followed by the first verse of a psalm, followed by " Glory be to the Father ", followed by the short sentence again. The short sentence is what is called an antiphon; if you come into chapel by mistake when the nuns are saying Office, you will find that they say an antiphon at the beginning of each psalm, and repeat it at the end. By rights, of course, the priest ought to say the whole psalm as part of the Introit. That would have meant, yesterday, that before getting on to *Kyrie eleison* I should have had to say the whole of the 118th psalm, which is 176 verses long. That would have made your breakfast very cold. But the Church, in her great kindness for our insides, has arranged that we should only say the first verse of the psalm, and then call it a day and go on with " Glory be to the Father ".

After that, probably, we ought to settle down and sing the Litany of the Saints. That's what happens if you go to Church on Holy Saturday; the Litany is sung, while the sacred ministers all lie flat on their faces on the altar steps. The same thing happens at an Ordination service. The Mass, on solemn occasions like that, has remained unchanged all down the centuries; and probably in very early times Mass was like that every day. If I said the Litany of the Saints every morning after the Introit, even if you were pretty nippy with the responses, that would add a good ten minutes on to the Mass, and breakfast would be getting colder than ever. So the Church has arranged another let-off; instead of saying the Litany we just say the *Kyrie eleison*, to remind us that the Litany ought to be there. I expect I really ought to be flat on my face. Anyhow, that is the mood we all ought to be in just then; we ought to be grovelling. Perhaps you will complain that we grovelled enough last Sunday. But I must remind you again, till we are all sick of it, that that beginning bit isn't really part of the Mass. The Introit begins the real Mass, and after the Introit we go on to the real grovel. The point is that whenever you approach Almighty God in prayer you ought to be bowled over, at the very start, by the thought of his unutterable greatness. Outside space, outside time, almighty, unconfined, incommunicable, without parts or passions—what *can* induce Almighty God to take any notice of us, to take any interest in whether we are saying Mass or not? We ought to feel like flies going round on the wheel of a tank; that's how we ought to start Mass, start all our worship of God. Don't start by thinking of him as a sort of cosy Friend waiting to listen to you and wanting to be told how abominably you were treated in geography class; that's all right for later on, but the first thing is to grovel.

So we say *Kyrie eleison*, which you won't find in your Latin grammars, because the words aren't Latin, they're Greek. I expect you know that in Greece and in the Balkan States and all over the near East—all the part that used to belong to the Turkish Empire and now seems to be getting mysteriously swallowed up by Soviet Russia while we look the other way—Mass is said not in Latin but in Greek. That is true, not only of the Eastern Christians who have been in schism for the last thousand years and don't acknowledge the Pope, but also of the Catholics who live in that part of the world; they are allowed to go on having Mass in Greek because they always have. The Greek habit, apparently, was just to go on saying, " Lord, have mercy on us ". It is only in the Latin Mass that the words *Christe eleison* have been introduced, so that the whole thing has got into a tidier sort of pattern; we say three *Kyrie eleisons* to God the Father, three *Christe eleisons* to our Blessed Lord, and then three *Kyrie eleisons* to the Holy Spirit. That means four *Kyrie eleisons* and one *Christe eleison* for me, two *Kyrie eleisons* and two *Christe eleisons* for the server, if we both remember to count right. But the general effect is meant to be just mercy, mercy, mercy—it's not so much that we ought to feel beasts because we are sinners, as that we ought to feel worms because we are creatures; however holy and pious we were, we should still want to start by telling Almighty God that he *is* Almighty God and we are a set of perfectly ridiculous creatures; when we have got that into our heads we have begun to get the situation clear.

Well, after that we begin to want a bit of cheering

up. And the thing we use to cheer us up is the *Gloria in excelsis.* Originally, it seems, that only happened on Christmas Day; it is really a Christmas hymn, and that is why it begins with the words the Angels said to the shepherds, " Glory to God in high heaven, and peace on earth to the men who are God's friends." That doesn't, by the way, mean the people who love God; it means the people whom God approves of. The rest of the hymn isn't a particularly Christmassy sort of affair, but that can't be helped; the important thing is that the great bulk of it is an appeal to our Incarnate Lord, as Incarnate, to make things all right for us. In the Middle Ages, it used to vary with the different feasts. On feasts of our Lady, for example, you sang " thou only art holy, thou who dost sanctify Mary, thou only art the Lord, who hast Mary for thy subject, thou only, Jesus Christ, art most high, who dost honour Mary with her crown ". But nowadays it has become one of the unalterable parts of the Mass; and the general point of it, coming where it does, is that we try to cheer ourselves up, after all the grovelling, by reminding ourselves and reminding Almighty God that human nature has been raised to something altogether higher, ever since our Lord took human nature upon himself, and that if we unite our prayers with the prayer of our Incarnate Lord, we can, in spite of everything, make our prayers worth looking at. And when, at the beginning of the *Gloria*, the priest parts his hands and raises them and then brings them together again with that sort of scooping motion, he is (as it were) inviting our Lord to become Incarnate and come down to earth, so that we may present ourselves to God in the power of his sacrifice.

After that, we don't talk to our Lord again till the *Agnus Dei*.

Originally, as I say, you only got the *Gloria* on Christmas Day. Then it was put in on all feast days and most Sundays; so that in practice you hardly ever get a Mass without it unless it's a black Mass or a day in Lent, or some other mournful occasion. And that is as it should be, because when it is a mournful occasion we like to go on grovelling, instead of trying to cheer ourselves up. But when we want to feel jolly, as we do on feast days or on Sundays, because Sundays are meant to be jolly in spite of letters home, we recover from the mood of depression we felt during the *Kyrie*, and start quite gaily on the Collects.

III

DOMINUS VOBISCUM, COLLECTS

And let all the people say, Amen. Ps. cv.

III

DOMINUS VOBISCUM, COLLECTS

And let all the people say, Amen. Ps. cv.

CARDINAL NEWMAN has a passage in one of his works which is generally quoted as his " description of a gentleman." I am not going to give you the whole of it, because you might think it was rather off the point; I don't think Cardinal Newman has given us anywhere a description of a lady. But the first sentence of it is this, " He has eyes on all his company ". That is not a bad thing to remember, even if you are a lady; always to remember who are the other people in the room, or are likely to be within earshot just outside the window, so as not to say the wrong thing; not to go on being boring if everybody is yawning behind their hands; trying as far as possible to bring everybody into the conversation, especially the people who are shy and won't talk at all unless they are given a lead. (I am thinking about the holidays now; here I know you all talk at the same time, which makes things simpler though not always quieter.) And when the priest has got to the end of the *Gloria*, he seems to get a sort of scruple that he's not behaving quite like a gentleman. He's been thinking so much about the glory of Almighty God, and our need for redemption by our Blessed Lord, that he's forgotten all about Mary Jane. There is Mary Jane behind him, being left out in the cold; and that mustn't be allowed to happen, so he turns round to bring her into the conversation. Before turning round, he bends down and kisses the altar. That is very natural, if you come to think of it; he nearly always does kiss the altar before he turns his back on it—not quite always; he doesn't, for example, before giving Communion. But you will see easily enough that it is a kind of polite gesture, saying to Almighty God, " Excuse me one moment; I must just turn around and say *Dominus vobiscum* to my friends, or they will think they are being neglected; you know I would like to be thinking about you all the time, and I am leaving a kiss on the altar to show you that I love you better than anything or anyone else ".

There are all sorts of morals you might derive from that. One is that we ought never to be satisfied with the state of our souls until we find that leaving off saying our prayers is a kind of wrench to us. And one is that if charity towards other people demands it we ought to be ready to stop our prayers at a moment's notice. But we haven't time for morals; we must get on with the Mass. In saying, " The Lord be with you ", the priest puts his hands apart, you will have noticed, as if he were helping to wind off an imaginary skein of wool, and then brings them together again. I don't know what the origin of that gesture is; it may have been simply a way of holding your skirts up in the old days when priests wore long chasubles that reached to the floor. But I think there's an obvious and rather charming significance about this latest movement in the dance. The priest, as he swirls round to make us feel at home, wants to include all of us in his greeting, and so he stretches his hands out wide, so as to include ALL the people who are in church; even the people who have been too lazy to get up early, because he is not allowed to lift his eyes from the ground when he turns towards the congregation, to prevent his getting distractions, so he can't tell whether you are actually there or in bed. But that nice comprehensive gesture of his asks the Lord to be with you, whether you are actually at Mass or not. So there are two reasons why you should feel rather pleased with yourself when the priest turns round and says *Dominus vobiscum.* It's nice that he should be thinking of us too, even when he is absorbed in an engrossing occupation like saying Mass. And it is nice that he should be thinking about all of us, and spread out his hands like that to shew that he's thinking about all of us. And we answer with the server, mentally, of course, *Et cum spiritu tuo.* Not ET CUM SPIRITUO, because that isn't Latin and isn't sense; there are two TU'S, Et cum spiriTU TUO. And that, as before, simply means " The same to you ".

Then he says *Oremus,* " Let us pray". And we are a bit inclined to be indignant, like the Lancashire man who was asked, " Wilt thou take this woman to thy wedded wife? " and answered, "Ah coom a purpose ". What's the good of saying " Let us pray " when we are praying already? I know . . . But were we? If you find that you are liable to have distractions when you are assisting at Mass, as most people do, and not only I'm afraid when they are assisting at Mass but when they are saying Mass, try this dodge. Make up your mind from the start that whenever the priest says *Oremus* you will shake yourself and say,

"Mary Jane, wake up". That will give you five jumps in the course of Mass; one when the priest goes up to the altar, one just before the Collects, one at the beginning of the Offertory, one just before the Our Father (which is the loveliest bit of Mass, I think) and one before the Post-Communion prayers.

By the time he says *Oremus* the priest has got his back to you again; he has gone back to the Epistle corner to find the book, because it's got the Collects and Epistle in it, and he doesn't know those by heart. The Epistle end of the altar has two purposes. All the rather less important things are done there, like the Offertory and the washing at the end, and at High Mass the blessing of the incense. And nearly all, but not quite all, of the bits that change from day to day are said at the Epistle corner. Why, I don't know. What is the idea of these Collects? Well, I think the nicest way to think about them is to think about them as a set of telegrams sent to Almighty God in honour of the occasion. You know how sometimes a few old school friends will meet out in Ceylon or Buenos Aires or somewhere to have a dinner, on some day which used to be a special feast day at their old school. And one thing they never fail to do; they always send a telegram to the headmaster to say FLOREAT NARKOVER, or whatever the name of their old school was. Just for once, now that they are together, they must send a joint message of salutation. And I think that is rather what the Collects at Mass are; just for once, now that we are all together, let us send a joint message of salutation to Almighty God; exiles, thinking about home. Some people think that is the reason why Collects are called Collects, because they were used at the *collecta*, the great meeting of Christian people for worship. I don't know. But there's another reason why I say they are like telegrams—they try to get a lot into a very little space. If you are in the habit of sending telegrams, you know how difficult it is to make them nice and cheap without at the same time making them very obscure. A Collect, like a telegram, ought to say what it wants to say in a very few words, and at the same time to be intelligible.

Unfortunately the books you have with you probably don't succeed in making the Collects intelligible, because they will try to translate them literally, and of course that makes them sound utter nonsense. This morning's was a fairly simple one, and you can't go far wrong with it; this, I think, is the sort of way it ought to be translated: " Lord, we beseech thee, guard this family of thine with a father's unfailing care; as it leans on thy heavenly grace for all its hope, so may it never lack the shelter of thy protection ". Nearly always in the Mass the Collect addresses God the Father, and asks that its petitions may be granted through the merits of our Blessed Lord, at the end.

When I've finished the Collect I don't go on to the Epistle, I start saying another Collect. And you rush through your book, remembering hard not to lick your finger before turning the pages, to find the part where the November saints come, because that's the likeliest guess. And, sure enough, about half way through the Epistle you get it; St. Martin, of course, it's St. Martin's day! The nice Roman soldier who gave away half of his overcoat to a beggar, and in a dream that night saw our Lord wearing it. St. Martin has had bad luck this year, because his feast fell on a

Sunday, so we can't say his Mass, we have to say the Sunday Mass instead. Or rather, it is we who have had bad luck; I don't suppose it makes much difference to St. Martin whether we keep his feast or not. But, just to show we haven't forgotten him, we put in a commemoration; we say his Collect immediately after the Collect of the day, and so with the Secret prayer and the Post-Communion prayer of his feast. We ask God that, as we have no legs of our own to stand on, we may be fortified against all dangers by the intercession of blessed Martin, his bishop and confessor. And even then we haven't finished. There was a hermit called Mennas who was martyred in Egypt on November 11, a bit over 1,600 years ago, and we still say an extra prayer to commemorate *him*. The Church has a long memory.

Supposing that St. Mennas had been martyred a day earlier, and St. Martin had died a day later, would we just say the Collect of the Sunday and leave it at that? No, if there's no important feast to be commemorated, we throw in two extra Collects for luck. At this time of year, the first of those two is a commemoration of all the saints from our Lady downwards. And the second the priest is allowed to choose for himself, out of a list of thirty-five different prayers which you will find in the missal just before the Mass for the dead. So it's no good asking the nuns beforehand about that, because the nuns can't possibly tell which of those thirty-five Collects I shall say. But I don't mind telling you that my favourite one, the one I usually say on such occasions, is the prayer *Pro devotis amicis*; and whether that means "for our devout friends", or "for our devoted friends",

I have never been able to find out. But it's a nice prayer: "O God, who by the grace of the Holy Spirit hast poured into the hearts of thy faithful the gifts of love; grant health of body and health of soul to those servants and hand-maids of thine for whom we implore thy mercy; that they may love thee with all their strength, and with all their love carry out thy will". If you are given your choice about which Collect you are going to say, it would be very hard to beat that.

All through this bit, the movements of the dance are rather complicated. The priest spreads out his hands when he says *Dominus vobiscum*, puts them together again, spreads them out again when he says *Oremus*, puts them together again, and then spreads them out again when he starts the Collect; what are we going to make of all that? Well, I think you can treat it as a sort of "Ready, steady, GO"; the *Dominus vobiscum* to wake you up, the *Oremus* to get you ready for action, and then the prayer itself. All through the prayers, as well as all through the Preface and most of the way through the Canon of the Mass, the priest holds his hands like that. I expect really he ought to be holding them wide out and high up, but nowadays the rubrics have reduced it to a mere gesture. Israel defeated the Madianites when Moses, with two friends to help him, kept his hands raised in prayer all through the battle. The point of the gesture is, surely, keeping yourself on the stretch. And the priest when he is saying the Collects is, so to speak, conducting an orchestra; you are the orchestra. He holds up his hands to tell you to keep it going, keep it going! Pray, pray hard; here's the whole world going to rack and ruin, here's the devil loose as he hasn't been for centuries, and the Church having to struggle and shout and starve to keep things going at all; pray hard, keep it up! And then you get to the words, " Through Jesus Christ our Lord . . ." and so on; and the priest puts his hands together again. There, that'll do, he says, you can stand down for a bit now. We've put it all in our Blessed Lord's hands; he is up there in Heaven with the Father and the Holy Spirit; he will see us through. And at that point the server mustn't forget to say, audibly and definitely, Amen. That is you, the congregation, saying " Hear, hear " at the end of my speech; that is you putting your signature to the telegram we are sending up to Almighty God, our S O S message praying for the needs of the Church.

IV

EPISTLE, GRADUAL, GOSPEL

Speak, Lord; thy servant is listening. I *Kings iii.*

IV

EPISTLE, GRADUAL, GOSPEL

Speak, Lord; thy servant is listening. I *Kings iii.*

AT THIS point in the Mass, we get on to something quite fresh; I mean, when we get on to the Epistle and Gospel. Everywhere else, nearly, we are talking to God, just now and again exchanging a *Dominus vobiscum*, or something of that kind, with one another. But in the Epistle and the Gospel we are letting God speak to us. It is an awful mistake to think that at this point we can take the thing easily; that we have heard all this hundreds of times before, and even if we hadn't we could always look it up; what is the sense of having that very long Gospel about the end of the world (it isn't about the end of the world really, it's about the destruction of Jerusalem) when we are all rather hungry for breakfast, which our insides are accustomed to taking at eight? All that is a mistake; we ought to follow the Epistle and Gospel on Sundays, anyhow, when it's read in English; why does the Church want it to be read in English if we don't listen to it? And even on week-days the Epistle and Gospel are worth following, though you may not want to follow the whole Mass. That is especially true in Lent, when we get a fresh Epistle and Gospel every day.

By the way, I forgot to tell you something.

Occasionally, but not often, and never on Sundays, you get things called " Prophecies " which come in between the *Kyrie eleison* and the Collects. If the *Gloria* is being said on a day of that kind, these Prophecies come before the *Gloria*. You can generally tell when it is happening, because there is generally a bit of a scrap between the priest and the server. Having got through the first Prophecy, the server says *Deo gratias*, and comes round and tries to take the book away from the priest, thinking that this is the end of the Epistle. And the priest has to explain that it is a false alarm, we haven't nearly got on to the Epistle yet. Sometimes there are quite a lot of them; on Holy Saturday there are twelve, and the last is a very long one, all about Nabuchodonosor and the band. Originally, I imagine, Mass always started with these long chunks of the Old Testament—the Prophecies always come from the Old Testament—to remind Christians of the origins they sprang from; to remind them that if they had still been Jews, instead of becoming Christians, they would have far longer and more frequent readings from the Old Testament, and it would have been much worse. I am not quite sure whether you will still be infesting the place on Wednesday the 19th; but if so you will come in for Prophecies at Mass, or rather for a single Prophecy. When I've finished the *Kyrie* I go straight over to the book, without any *Dominus vobiscum*, and say *Flectamus genua*, which means " Let us bend our knees ", genuflecting as I do so. And the person who is answering, if it's somebody terrifically on the spot, will answer *Levate*, which means " Get up ". That sounds rather rude, but it's not meant that way;

in theory we ought all to be genuflecting, and of course with those rather crowded seats it would be very uncomfortable if you had to stay genuflected for long, so the server says " Get up ". Then I read a rather jolly bit of Isaias, and rather topical just now: " They will melt down their swords into ploughshares, their spears into pruning-hooks, nation levying war against nation and training itself for battle no longer. Come you too (they will say), children of Jacob, let us walk together where the Lord shews us light." And then there is a verse or two from the psalms, and we go on to the *Dominus vobiscum* and the Collects.

But, as I say, that only happens now and again. The Epistle always happens; what exactly is the point of it? Well, I told you that the Collects were rather like telegrams sent off as a demonstration of loyalty; and I think the Epistle is rather like a letter, as indeed you would expect from its name; I mean, the kind of letter that is written from a long distance away, perhaps from a son in China or somewhere, and consequently has to be read out for the benefit of the whole family at breakfast. Letters in the old days used to arrive in time for breakfast, and in the old days we used to listen to them being read out—we didn't just sit there and say, " Hurry up with that letter, Pop, I want the stamp ". It happens, sometimes, at public gatherings; one of the people on the platform gets up and reads out a letter from the Prime Minister or somebody like that. And sometimes, of course, the bishop sends round a letter that has to be read out in all the parish churches; at the beginning of Advent, for instance. Next Sunday, if you got your deserts, you would have eight or nine pages from the Bishop of Shrewsbury read out at Mass, and your breakfast would be further off than ever. Only we don't do that, partly because this isn't exactly a parish church, and partly because the Bishop is a very nice man, who doesn't fuss one about those things.

Well, of course, that's what St. Paul's letters were; they were addressed not to individuals, Tychicus or Trophimus or Mary Jane, but to a whole local congregation, and no doubt they were read out at Mass; though I hope the Epistle to the Romans was taken in sections, or breakfast must have got very cold indeed. And I suppose, if you come to think of it, they have gone on being read out in church from that day to this. That Epistle we had this morning was part of a letter St. Paul wrote to the Christians at Colossae, about A.D. 60; and I suppose the Colossians said, "That's rather a jolly bit, let's have that again next Sunday"; and then somehow it got into the calendar and we still read it every year, as a kind of pastoral Epistle from St. Paul to us, as if St. Paul were still alive and still living at Rome. And because it's all such a family affair, reading out loud a letter we have just received from the dear apostle, we slack off a bit. Everything, you notice, goes slack at the Epistle. At High Mass, when there is one of those long Sequences before the Gospel, the priest may go and sit down, if he likes; and even at Low Mass, though he doesn't sit down, he is behaving rather casually—while the Epistle and the things which immediately follow it are being read, the priest just hangs on to the edge of the book. That is the only part of the Mass, if you come to think of it, where the priest isn't holding his hands joined, or spread apart, or in some other artificial position dictated to him by the rubrics. When the Epistle comes, he stands easy; just puts his hands anyhow.

So let's try and think of the Epistle, always, as a personal letter sent to us from St. Paul, or one of the other apostles, who is a long way away, but still very much interested in us. Take that Epistle this morning—there's nothing there, I think, St. Paul wouldn't be wanting to say, isn't wanting to say, to you or me. "We have been praying for you," he says, "unceasingly"; of course he has; the saints in Heaven go on praying all the time, and they pray for all Christian people. He has been praying that you and I may have a closer knowledge of God's will; that you and I may live as God's servants, waiting continually on his pleasure; that you and I may be inspired with full strength, to be patient and to endure; isn't that nice of him? We feel inclined to say "Hurrah!" at the end of it; only we don't say it; we just think "Hurrah!" when the server says *Deo gratias*.

I don't think we'll worry much about the short prayers that come just after the Epistle. They really belong to sung Mass; and in old days the sacred ministers just sat there and fanned themselves while the choir had its day out; there was no business of people bowing to one another and carting candles about while the choir was singing. In old days, too, it was a full psalm; we should have had twenty-six verses of Gradual this morning. It was called the Gradual because the man who intoned the psalm was mounted on a high step; Latin, *gradus*, a step. Of course it is sung very gradually indeed, in churches where they sing plainchant; but that has got nothing to do with it. At Low Mass, it helps by giving the server time to come round and take the book away *after* the priest has looked round and caught his eye, or laid his hand on the altar, as some priests do. I forgot to mention that that gesture is the only gesture in the Mass which isn't prescribed by the rubrics; it's just a private hint to shew that the Epistle is over.

And then the Gospel. The most obvious thing about the Gospel is that it is read at the wrong side of the altar, at its northern end; nothing ever happens there at Mass except the Gospel and the last Gospel. One is apt to be a little surprised at that, because the Gospel is obviously of terrific importance in the Mass, so why should it always be sung or said on the left-hand side? The answer to that, I think, is that it is really the right-hand side. You are thinking of it as the left-hand side because it is on the priest's left. But you ought to think of the altar as God's throne; you ought to learn, in this and everything else, to look at things from God's point of view. Think of God sitting throned over the altar, with our Blessed Lord on his right hand, and you will see why the Gospel of Jesus Christ is read out from that side. Or think of the crucifix which stands over the altar —it was on our Lord's right, according to the pictures, that the Penitent Thief was crucified; and that explains why the Gospel of pardon is read just there. At High Mass, there is a great deal of ceremonial here, and a procession with candles and incense, and the sub-deacon turning himself into a sort of human reading-desk, so that the deacon can get a good look.

At Low Mass the thing is all rather telescoped, but you can tell something important is happening all the same.

The priest prepares himself for the reading of the Gospel by saying two prayers, as he bows to the Cross on his way over from one side to the other. They both ask that he may have the right kind of heart and the right kind of lips for proclaiming the holy Gospel. In theory, you see, the deacon or priest who reads out the Gospel is doing what the Christian ministry exists to do before everything else—he is preaching Christ. I always wonder whether the idea of the Gospel being read at the north end of the chancel may not have been partly due to the fact that Christianity started in the south; I mean, it was the south of the known world. Our religion started in Palestine, spread in Asia Minor and round the Mediterranean. For a long time, it seemed like a kind of Polar expedition to preach the Gospel of Christ to Russians, or Germans, or the inhabitants of Britain. All those dreadful heathen people up in the cold north—perhaps that was how the deacon was meant to think of it, as he shouted the day's Gospel at the northern wall of the sanctuary. And I think it is a good thing for us, when we see him doing that, to reflect on God's mercy in calling us, calling improbable people like us, to be Christians.

In order to preach the Gospel well, the ministers of Christ want to have pure hearts and pure lips. Pure hearts, because in proportion as their consciences reproach them with the kind of life they are living, the kind of thoughts they are thinking, in that proportion they will feel false inside, and to feel false inside means a want of conviction about the handing on of your message. Pure lips, because it is on the whole by what we say, and the way in which we say it, that other people judge our characters; and if the priest is given to backbiting, to outbursts of anger in his speech, to boasting, to flattery, to grousing, to lying, to blasphemy, to unseemly talk, he is not likely to impress the people who listen to his sermons. That does not apply only to the clergy. Every Christian is preaching Christ, every day, by the life he or she lives, by the words he or she utters, from day to day; you are all the time unconsciously influencing other people. Don't try to influence other people CONSCIOUSLY, to talk good and put on airs of goodness; it will only turn you into a prig, and your friends will see through it. Try to live near to our Lord; get inside the thought of what his words mean, live on that model, so that you may be a friend of his, so that you may be the kind of person he feels at home with. Then, unconsciously, you will influence other people. In this nasty, wind-swept world, in which charity has gone cold and there is a frost of winter all about us, your life will be a glow of love; a faint glow, perhaps, but one at which other people can just warm their hands. Now, at the beginning of it, say *Gloria tibi, Domine,* as the server says at the beginning of the Gospel; try and dedicate it, the whole of it, to God's glory. Then, when you come to the end of it, your last thoughts will be of thankfulness for having been allowed to live it, and you will say *Laus tibi, Christe,* as the server says at the end of the Gospel, "Praise be to thee, O Christ".

V

CREDO

What I was born for, what I came into the world for, is to bear witness of the truth. John xviii.

V

CREDO

What I was born for, what I came into the world for, is to bear witness of the truth. John xviii.

THE *Credo* is a curious feature of the Mass, and I expect we shall probably have to devote a whole sermon to it. As you know, it is not an essential feature of the Mass; it only comes on certain big days. On all Sundays and all feasts of our Lord, our Lady, St. Joseph or the holy Angels; on feasts of the apostles and evangelists, because they spread the faith, and on feasts of doctors, because they defended the faith and explained it to us. Also on frightfully important patronal feasts, and on St. Mary Magdalen's day. I daresay that a thousand years hence the Church will be saying it at every Mass, and learned people will be inventing ingenious explanations of why it wasn't said every day in remote times like the twentieth century.

It wasn't, by the way, till the eleventh century, that is, Norman Conquest, 1066, that the Creed was said at Mass in the Roman rite at all. When you come to think of it, it's not so obvious why we do say it. I mean, at the baptism service the Creed comes in (although it's the other Creed) quite naturally. At the very start, you tell the infant that if it is going to be a member of the Christian Church it has got to keep the commandments, and it howls pretty dismally at that. When you have finished the business in the porch and take the infant to the font, you add, And, by the way, you've got to believe all the following statements, and repeat the Creed to it, at which it howls worse than ever. But then, you see, you've got an unbeliever in the church; at Mass, there may be one or two unbelievers who have come in to hear the sermon or the Mozart Mass, but surely the Church isn't going to worry about them? Since we are practically all believers and wouldn't be there if we weren't believers, what is the sense of holding up business to remind ourselves about the things we believe?

Well, I think the most important answer is this—you have come to Mass to worship God, and that means worshipping God with your whole being, not just with bits of it. Worship doesn't mean merely letting your feelings go out to God, telling him how good he is and getting all worked up about your sins; doesn't mean merely letting your will go out to God, resolving that you are going to live for him and resigning yourself to all the uncomfortable things he may ask you to suffer for him. It means also letting your intellect go out to God, telling him that he exists, that he is utterly above your comprehension, and that he has revealed himself in Jesus Christ so as to make it possible for you to comprehend him a little. That is why I have taken my text from that passage we all know, but don't always reflect on, in St. John. The reason why I was born, our Lord tells Pilate, was—what? So as to save the world? So as to heal the sick and give sight to the blind? So as to comfort people who were unhappy? No, so as to tell the truth, so as to bear witness of the truth. That is man's first need; he is a reasonable animal, and he must know what he is and where he stands before he can sit down and be satisfied. And that is man's first duty; to think, and to think right. As part of your worship of him, God demands that you should let your intellect travel on the right lines in thinking about him. Very likely it is not much of an intellect, and shews strong signs of throwing up the sponge when it gets to recurring decimals. But it's the best intellect you've got, and it is all meant to be put at God's disposal.

I've told it you lots of times, but I'm going to say it again, truth does matter. Saying the right thing doesn't merely mean saying what's kind, it means saying what's true. If you thought this an interesting sermon, and came up to me afterwards to say, "What a boring sermon that was!" it would be a bad thing to do. It would be a bad thing to do because your words wouldn't be doing justice to your thought. If you think this a boring sermon, and come up to me afterwards to say, "What an interesting sermon that was!" it might be all very well for me, it might send me back to translating Paralipomenon with a lighter heart, but it would still be a bad thing to do, because your words wouldn't be doing justice to your thought. And so it is with dishonesty, cheating about marks, for example; so it is with lying of every kind. Of course, it is worse to cheat over marks if there is an exam on, and it may gain you an unfair advantage. Of course it's worse to tell a lie if it means letting other people down. But even when there is nothing much to be gained, when there is not much harm to be done, cheating or lying is wrong because it is warping your own moral nature. You are, if I may put it in that way, preventing yourself growing up. Kids lie, because they think it's something clever; how would you like to be called a kid? But you are, you know, if you encourage yourself in dishonest habits of mind; you are refusing to grow into the full stature of a woman; you are keeping a kind of soft spot in your mind which disgraces the image of God.

So, when you assist at a Mass where the *Credo* is said, there is something for you to think about. Tell Almighty God, "I know what I was born for, I know what I came into the world for; to bear witness of the truth. I can never really be a partaker of the Divine nature, Jesus Christ can never be on easy terms with me, until I have learned to see things as they are and to call things by their right names. And the most important kind of truth is the truth you have revealed to us; I want to let my mind be carried away by it, because that is one of the ways in which it is possible for me to worship you; indeed, it is the first thing I have got to do, if I am going to worship you. This and this and this I believe to be true, because you have told me that they are true; and although my mind can only take these truths in very imperfectly, because it's such a silly mind, I want it to be carried away by these truths, penetrated by these truths; I want it to chime in with these truths, as instinctively as my voice chimes in with the note that is given on the harmonium. Then my intellect, as well as the rest of me, will be worshipping you."

But, of course, there is a perfectly different question which, for all I know, you are dying to ask—Why should the *Credo* come in just here? I am sure there are lots of learned books that would enable me to answer that question, but I haven't got them, and I don't know. All I know is that some of the other rites in the Christian Church don't put it in in the same place. If you went to Mass in a certain chapel of the cathedral at Toledo, or in a certain chapel of the cathedral at Salamanca, which are both places in Spain, you would hear Mass said according to the Mozarabic rite; that is to say, you would hear a perfectly good Catholic Mass at which the *Credo* was said after the Consecration and before the Communion. So it's probably more or less of an accident that in our ordinary Roman rite it got stuck where it did. But I think on the whole it was a fortunate accident, if it was one; I think it is rather a jolly place to have it. For this reason; that if you follow the Gospel it is rather apt to drive you in on yourself; and the *Credo* helps to take you out of yourself; to make you see yourself as a very small and unimportant detail against a flaming background of eternal truth.

If you come to think of it, we are most of us a bit too self-centred; you are too apt to catch sight of yourself, if I may put it in that way, out of the corner of your eye. Most of us find that our thoughts, if we aren't careful, return too easily on ourselves; it's all right if we are watching a flick, or reading a detective story or something really gripping; but if we sit down to read about the kings of England it isn't long before we find that our attention has wandered back to Mary Jane. No, it's all right; I'm not going to scold you about having distractions in your prayers; for one thing I never do scold people about that, and for another thing that's not what I'm talking about. No, but if you follow the Gospel it is apt to make you think about YOU; the Gospel is so full of scoldings for rather second-rate Christians like you and me; some phrase of it sticks, and we feel dissatisfied with ourselves, and inclined to brood over it. And we fall to wondering why it is that the people round us, who after all have the best opportunity of judging, seem to think so poorly of us; as if it mattered a brass farthing what anybody except Almighty God thinks of us . . . And when we are in that rather self-centred, rather self-pitying mood, we need a bit of a jolt to take us out of ourselves. And the jolt that takes you out of yourself is the priest saying quite suddenly *Credo in unum Deum.* It always does come rather suddenly, doesn't it? At High Mass, it seems to take about half a minute while the organist is putting his music straight and the choir are clearing their throats before they can get on with the tune; as if this sudden announcement that the priest believes in one God had taken them all by surprise.

When you get a priest who really does his ceremonies well—and that must be a great relief, after me—he stands quite still and bolt upright during the first part of the *Credo.* I always feel I want to sway from side to side, and I expect I do. Because this part is so exciting; it's something almost more profane than a dance. Do you ever watch people playing Rugby football? Sometimes you will see a really good man get away with the ball and run for the touch-line, swaying from this side to that so as to make it more difficult for people to tackle him, and fending people off, first on this side then on that, when they try to interfere with him. That is

AUGUSTANA THEOLOGICAL
SEMINARY LIBRARY
ROCK ISLAND, ILLINOIS

what this first part of the *Credo* is like. It is the Catholic Church of Christ keeping its poise, resisting the onslaughts of heresy, first on this side, then on that, preserving the perfect balance of the faith and making straight for the goal. One God, the Father, the All-powerful, Creator of heaven and earth, of all things seen and unseen. One God; splendid; we've got that. And in one Lord, Jesus Christ . . . what exactly do you mean by Lord? Isn't Lord the same as God? Wait a moment; God's begotten Son; the only Son; yes, we are all sons of God, but this is the only Son who can claim God, in the strict sense, as his Father. We belong to time; he was begotten of his Father before time began. A paradox? Of course it is, to us; that act, not of creation but of Divine procreation, by which the Second Person of the Trinity has being, is eternal, with the eternity of God himself; there never was a time when *he* did not exist.

Why, then, he must be the *same* as God; there can't be two different Beings like that . . . Wait a moment; God sprung from God, Light sprung from Light; tell me whether the sunlight is the same as the sun, or something different from the sun, then I will tell you how God can be sprung from God, and yet there is only one God still. The same in substance with the Father, a different Person, yet one with him in Godhead. By whom all things were made; we said just now that the First Person of the Blessed Trinity was creator of all things, now we say that all things were made by the Second Person of the Blessed Trinity; I and my Father are one, he told us; my Father is at work all the time, and I, I too am at work. The Arian heretics, you see, maintained that the Second

Person of the Trinity was *created*; well, answers the Church, it's odd if that is so; he must have created himself.

. . . And then you get a fresh, sudden transition. Who for us, for us men, for our salvation, for the ridiculously unimportant salvation of ridiculously unimportant people like us, CAME DOWN FROM HEAVEN. Can you wonder that at that point the priest falls on his knees? *You* weren't following, of course, you were day-dreaming, and so you were taken by surprise, just like the organist at the *Credo in unum Deum*; if the girl behind you hadn't suddenly butted you with her nose in the small of the back, it's arguable that you would have forgotten to go down on your knees at all. But really, of course, the whole mood of the melody has changed. You are now thinking of the Second Person of the Blessed Trinity as Incarnate, as Man, as our Representative, offering, as Man, to his Father, as God, that eternal sacrifice which we now come to commemorate, with which we now mean to associate ourselves. If you are really following, you will see that the *Credo* has come just at the right moment. It has taken our attention away from Mary Jane, swept it up into the most baffling and the most august mysteries of theology, only to bring it back again to where it started from, God come down to earth, and Mary Jane redeemed.

VI

OFFERTORY I

Whence shall we ? John vi.

VI

OFFERTORY I

Whence shall we? John vi.

I DIDN'T say nearly all there is to say about the *Credo*, the Sunday before last, but I think we had better take it as said and go on to the Offertory, because we don't seem to be getting through the Mass as quickly as we ought to. At the end of the *Credo*, the priest turns and says *Dominus vobiscum*, and then *Oremus*. Don't be taken in by that; it's a false alarm. The priest says *Oremus*, Let us pray—and then he doesn't do anything of the sort; he just starts doing things with the chalice and paten. But on the whole I think it's rather a good thing that the priest does kid you like that; because as I was saying before the word *Oremus* is a useful sort of alarm-clock (if we will use it like that) to wake us up at various points in the Mass, just when our attention was in danger of going to sleep. And it generally means something is going to happen; a new movement in the dance is just going to begin. On being invited to pray like that, you immediately sit down, to shew that you are not being taken in. But the fact that you are sitting down doesn't mean that it's a good moment for exchanging a word with a friend, or joggling that loose tooth in the hope that it will come out, or otherwise just filling in the time. The Offertory is really rather an important part of the Mass, and all the more so because, in a sense, this is where you come on.

I rather think if you go to High Mass in a Dominican church you will find that point emphasized; I mean about the Offertory being important. The Dominicans, as I dare say you know, have a rite of their own when they say Mass. It was only in 1570, you see, that St. Pius V, the same Pope who excommunicated Queen Elizabeth, said it was really time we stopped saying Mass more or less as we liked, and the whole of Latin Christendom must say it in the same way. But, he added, that wasn't to apply to religious orders who had been using a rite of their own for two hundred years or more; and that included the Dominicans. I may tell you, in a sort of undertone, that St. Pius V was a Dominican himself. And that's why when Father Gerald Vann comes here he not only wears odd clothes but says Mass in such an unexpected way. In certain of the old rites too there is a lot of ceremonial leading up to the Offertory. The chalice and paten haven't been in church at all up till then; and at the *Dominus vobiscum—Oremus* a procession comes out of the sacristy, with the subdeacon carrying the chalice and paten, and people walking with candles and so on in front of him. It all seems rather overdone to us, perhaps because we are accustomed to do things much more simply; and at Low Mass all that happens is that two wretched little boys in red cassocks scramble to their feet and go round to the side and have a quarrel about which shall hold the water and which the wine. What's the sense of making a fuss about it?

Well, in the first place I think you can say this; the Mass is all one; the sacrifice is going on all the time, not just at odd intervals. We pick out certain bits of it and treat them as high spots; there's a bell for the *Sanctus*, bells for the Consecration, bells for the *Domine non sum dignus*; and if we aren't careful we shall think of the Mass as three separate moments of action with a few odd prayers shoved in between. That, of course, is all wrong; the Mass is a continuous action; and I expect most of you have been brought up to realize that from the Preface down to the priest's Communion the sacrifice is being made. What I mean is that it's not like hanging on to the telephone and waiting for a call to come through, suddenly; it's like watching a game of tennis, say, at which every stroke counts. And I think it's much more business-like to treat the Offertory, not the Preface, as the starting point; though I don't know if people who are learned in liturgy would back me up there. *I* think the continuous action of the Mass begins just here, with the Offertory.

It's all very well for you to point out that the Offertory is only concerned with unconsecrated bread and wine, and that isn't much to get excited about. That's quite true, of course, but I think if you will use your imagination for a moment you will see that there is good excuse for making a lot of the unconsecrated host, the unconsecrated chalice. They may have no great importance of their own at the moment, but they are *going* to be terrifically important. And it's very narrow-minded of us if we think only of what things are at the moment, not of what they are going to be.

Imagine yourself walking through a field of wheat; out in the park, say, by the deer-cote. All those ears of wheat are full of promise; they are going to be something. That particular ear of wheat which is sticking out on the left of the path will be threshed, ground in the mill, baked in the oven, made into a sandwich, and be eaten by somebody on a railway journey; that is the destiny which is shaping itself inside that particular set of little husks. Now look at that ear of wheat which is sticking out on the right of the path. That one will be threshed, ground in the mill—the same mill, baked in the oven—no, not in the same oven, or at any rate, not in the same batch; there will be no baking powder this time. Then it will be pressed by a Carmelite nun in a press which will give it the imprint of the crucifix; it will be sent off in a tin to the sacristan of some church; it will lie on the altar, some Latin words will be said over it, and after that it will be lifted up in a gold monstrance, and everybody who passes in front of it will go down on both knees . . . It's the same with the chalice, only, of course, we aren't so familiar with the process of making wine. That cluster over there will find its way into a bottle of ordinary wine; somebody will drink it over his dinner; get drunk on it, perhaps, and come to blows, and be sent to prison. That other cluster will find its way into a bottle of altar wine, will be consecrated, will be drunk by a priest, and bring him just the grace he needed to resist that temptation, to rise to that height of sanctity. And yet the two clusters grew side by side in the same vineyard, long ago.

So what the priest is doing at the altar is to separate, to earmark, this particular lump of wheat, this particular dose of grape-juice, for a supernatural destiny.

And that, of course, is just what is happening to you and me all the time. Sooner or later we shall die, and that moment of death will be, please God, our Consecration; we shall be changed into something different, be given a spiritual body in place of our natural body, and live praising God among the Saints to all eternity. What we are doing now, all the time, is to make of our lives an Offertory to Almighty God; to separate them, set them apart for him, so that when death comes it may be our Consecration. And that is why the pious books will tell you, at the Offertory, to put yourself in imagination on the paten, between the priest's hands. You at the moment, your body at this moment, is something ridiculously cheap and unimportant; open one artery of it, choke up one air-passage for a few minutes, and it is done for; it will be buried away in the ground and rot there. That's what it is, but the point is not what it is but what it's going to be. Please God, when it has been consecrated as he means it to be consecrated—and he has all that planned out for you and me already—it is going to be a glowing focus of his praise, a mirror which will reflect his uncreated loveliness, for all eternity.

We mustn't despise, then, the unconsecrated host which the priest is holding up in front of the crucifix, the drops of wine which are trickling down into the chalice; we must think of what they are going to be. You have all of you heard about good King Wenceslas, because a clergyman wrote a rather inaccurate carol about him, which thousands of people will be singing this next fortnight. You know all about his making the page carry pine-logs to the poor man's house, although as it was right against the forest fence, you would have thought it would have been simpler to chop him up a dead branch or two on the spot. What you don't know is that King Wenceslas always insisted on making the altar-breads for his chapel with his own hands, because he thought even a king ought to be proud to do that. And the whole idea of the Offertory is that the bread and wine are something which YOU hand over to ME, which the laity hand over to the priest, to see what he can make of them. That's why I say that this is the point where YOU come in. Those two small boys in red cassocks, one of them with hiccoughs and the other with his shoe-lace undone, represent you, represent the congregation. In theory, you are all crowding on to the sanctuary, turning the priest's solitary dance into a tumultuous round-dance; all holding out pieces of bread and shouting, " Father Knox! Father Knox! Do bless this one! " That's what the Offertory really is; only you aren't actually expected to do quite that. You are expected to place your body, in imagination, beside the host on the paten, and to say, " Dear God, this ridiculous thing is all I have to offer you; please make something of it, if even you can make something even of a person like me ".

Yes, let us get excited about the unconsecrated bread and wine, because of what they are going to be; but don't let's lose sight of the fact that what they are going to be depends entirely on what God is going to do with them; WE could wave them about in the air and repeat Latin sentences over them from morning to night, and they would be just ordinary bread and wine still; it's only because God is going to take a hand that they are going to become something quite different. I always like to think of the Offertory as a repetition of what happened when our Lord fed the five thousand people in the wilderness, just with five loaves and a couple of fishes. That's why I took those words as my text, " Whence shall we? " Here are five thousand people all hungry and shouting for food, whence shall we, with only a few coppers in the common purse, buy two hundred pennyworth of bread, in a trackless desert where there are no bakers' shops anyhow? And then the shamefaced afterthought; " As a matter of fact there is an urchin here "—yes, an urchin; the word is only twice used in the New Testament, in Matthew xi where it means a guttersnipe, and here in John vi where it means an urchin—" an urchin who has five loaves and two small fishes; but *that* isn't going to go far among five thousand ". All the same, the urchin is produced, and stands there on one leg with his thumb in the corner of his mouth looking up at our Lord and grinning: " You can have them if you want." That is the server at Mass; the boy in the red cassock with hiccoughs who provides the priest with the material for the miracle that is just going to be performed in his hands. A pathetically small ration, but it's something; our Lord only wants us to give him something. Everything we do for him, every aspiration of our hearts towards him, is so ridiculously inadequate, considered in itself; it is his grace, really, that has got to do the miracle, to make something out of our efforts. Everything you and I do is just water for him to turn into wine, five rolls for him to feed a mass meeting with.

You see, then, something of what the Offertory is. *Suscipe, sancte Pater*, the priest says; " Holy Father, almighty, eternal God, receive this unspotted Victim" —he calls it that already! It is only a plain piece of bread, but because of what it is going to become, later on, he already calls it "the unspotted Victim"; the action of the Mass is all continuous, you see, and the action of the Mass has begun. On to that victim he piles all his innumerable sins, faults, and pieces of negligence; you wouldn't believe how many of them a priest has. On to that victim, he piles the needs of all the congregation present, nay, of all faithful Christians, living and dead; this piece of bread, which might equally well have been made into a sandwich and eaten in a railway train, is going to be the Victim that will bring us all to everlasting life. And then the chalice; the wine first, and then the tiny spot of water. If the priest, by mistake, puts into the chalice one eighth as much water as he has put wine, he must start all over again; the water has got to be a tiny spot. And the words the priest says as he does it give the explanation of that: "O God, by whom the worth of our human nature was wondrously fashioned, and refashioned more wondrously still, grant us, through the power of this water-mingled-with-wine, in imitation of this water-mingled-with-wine, to be partakers of his Godhead who was courteous enough to share our Manhood." Make us one and the same thing with Jesus Christ, our identity merged and lost in his, just as the identity of that spot of water is merged and lost in the wine that covers the bottom of the chalice. That is the whole point of the Offertory; to remind us how little it is we offer, so that when we get to the Consecration we may be bowled over, more than ever, by the thought of what he makes of it.

VII

OFFERTORY II

I appeal to you by God's mercies to offer up your bodies as a living sacrifice, consecrated to God and worthy of his acceptance; this is the worship due from you as rational creatures. Rom. xii. 1.

VII

OFFERTORY II

I appeal to you by God's mercies to offer up your bodies as a living sacrifice, consecrated to God and worthy of his acceptance; this is the worship due from you as rational creatures. Rom. xii. 1.

WE DIDN'T really finish, last time, about the Offertory at Mass; we just got down to the prayer which the priest says when he puts wine and water in the chalice. There are three more prayers he has to say before he goes back again to the side to wash his hands. I think they are a very good illustration of what we have been calling the dance of the Mass. If you got hold of an intelligent Mohammedan, and asked him to watch this bit of the Mass, and tell you what he made of it, I don't think he would go far wrong. He would say, " The mullah is now holding up a cup, as if he were offering it, with its contents, to somebody up in the air, a little way in front of him . . . Now he is standing there with his eyes downcast, in a humble attitude, as if he were rather ashamed, after all, of his gift . . . Now he is looking up at the sky and seems to be scooping down some kind of blessing on the cup, as if to make it all right." He has got the hang of the thing, more or less, from seeing it done in dumb show. You and I, who can read Latin and can find our way about the missal, could tell him that the words which the mullah is using are something very much to the same effect.

The first prayer is, " Lord, we offer thee the cup that is pledge of our salvation, and we ask thy indulgence for it; may it go up, up into the presence of thy Divine Majesty, and carry an acceptable fragrance with it ". We are using the language of the old Jewish sacrifices; under the Mosaic law you were always burning the carcases of animals, or at any rate the fat parts of them; and as you watched the thick black smoke go up to the sky you told yourself, " This fragrance will be acceptable to God "; it was a kind of technical term. You see, the Jews, who had only a very imperfect revelation made to them, were allowed to think of Almighty God as enjoying a good smell of cooking. Not that, as a matter of fact, the smell of fat burning is a particularly acceptable thing to *our* nostrils; it rather makes one want to open the window. But either the Jews liked their meat very well done, or else they must have argued that when you were cooking something in God's honour you couldn't cook it too thoroughly. The odd thing, I think, is this. In those old Jewish sacrifices the blood wasn't left in the victims that were put on the altar; it was drained away at the altar's foot. And yet we say this prayer about " acceptable fragrance ", not over the sacred host, but over the chalice whose contents will be, a few minutes from now, the Precious Blood. I have no idea why that is. Possibly it was just the smell of the wine—wine always smells very strong when you are fasting, as the priest is at Mass—suggested the idea of bringing in that tag from the old Law, though in a different context.

But simply because we don't know—or I don't know—how this particular phrase got into the Mass in the first instance, that is no reason why you and I shouldn't get plenty of juice out of it, when we are simply trying to think of a way in which we can follow the Mass devotionally. How would this do? When we were talking about the priest offering up the sacred host on the paten, we said that we would put ourselves, in imagination, on the paten too, and offer up ourselves to God in union with what the priest is doing. Our bodies, our souls, all that we are, as a gift. How would it be if we accompanied the priest's offering of the chalice with an offering to God of the destiny that awaits us, of the good fortune and the misfortune he means to send us; in fact, of our lives?

You see, that is a perfectly good Hebrew metaphor. It keeps on cropping up in the psalms, " this shall be the portion of their cup ", " the Lord himself is the portion of my inheritance, and of my cup "; the Jews thought of life, obviously, as a cup with some sweet draughts in it and some bitter draughts in it, but God put it to your lips and said, " Here, drink that ", with the authoritative tone the doctor uses when he gives you a medicine, and you have no choice but to accept it. I suppose we may say that our Blessed Lord, in taking human nature upon himself, took a Hebrew mind. He wouldn't have been human if he hadn't belonged to one particular nation. And because he spoke one particular language, Aramaic, because he was familiar with the literature of one people above all, the people of the Jews, his thought naturally clothed itself in the Jewish way. And so, when he knelt in Gethsemani, and breathed such a human prayer as staggers us, when we reflect that he who offered it was himself personally God, the language of that prayer, the thought of that prayer, was the language, was the thought of his own people. And he said, " Father, if it be possible, let this CUP pass from me ". The cup of our salvation was a bitter cup for him to drink. And when the priest asks God to accept the cup of salvation, shall we think about the cup which our Lord thought about in Gethsemani, and offer up our lives with it, as he offered up his life in Gethsemani: " Nevertheless, not my will, but thine, be done! "

When I have said that, let me qualify it by drawing your attention to a mistake we are all apt to make when we talk about offering things up. We are all apt to imagine that it only means offering up unpleasant things. It has become a part of our Catholic slang, hasn't it, to talk about " offering it up " in that special way; when the worst comes to the worst, and only then, you decide to offer it up. You offer up the cold you've got, and the pudding you don't like, and the length of the prep you've been set, and the ladders in your stockings, and the fountain-pen that won't write, and the earwig you find in the bath, and the window that rattles in your dormitory, and the other girl bagging the hot-water pipes first, and the noun in E mute that turns out to be masculine after all—offer them up, offer them up. If you want to be really rude to one of your friends who has annoyed you, there's no better way of getting your own back than telling her after Benediction that you've been offering her up. We even think of it, don't we, as a last resort; if you have a toothache you try putting oil of cloves on it, and if that doesn't work you take a couple of aspirins, and if that doesn't work you offer it up. It's a queer way to treat Almighty God, isn't it? Never to think about his will except when we're down and out? Our Lord, in Gethsemani, didn't suddenly remember that his heavenly Father had a will, and that will must be the best. He had been doing his heavenly Father's will, adoring his heavenly Father's will, at every moment of his life, in sunshine and in cloud alike, and his prayer in Gethsemani was simply the continuation of a prayer which had started in the manger at Bethlehem and never stopped.

Of course I know there are some of us who seem to find that the whole of life is just a series of set-backs; and if you are like that there is nothing to do but go on offering up the unpleasant things. Those of us who find it less monotonous than that ought surely to offer up to God the WHOLE chalice of our lives, the sweet draughts as well as the bitter. When we get a holiday or a recompense or when we get rid of a chilblain, we ought to offer up those moments to him just as much as the others. At Christmas time we ought to want to share our presents with the Baby Jesus: " What have they given you? Gold and frankincense and myrrh? I got a concertina "—that sort of thing. Sometimes when holy people, especially religious, want to be very kind to you, they give you a spiritual bouquet, so many Masses heard, Communions made, prayers offered, and so many sacrifices for one's intentions. It is always understood that the sacrifices are unpleasant things, isn't it? But I hope if you ever give me a spiritual bouquet, you will include a whole lot of the other sort of thing too;

so many ice-creams eaten, so many gramophone records played, so many visits to the pictures, for my intentions. Because then I shall feel you are offering the WHOLE of your lives to God.

I'm sorry to go on and on about that so, but it is a subject I see red about. When the priest stands holding up the chalice in front of him like that, your attitude should be one of holding out your life to Almighty God and offering it to him like that, the bitter and the sweet alike. After all, he is the good Physician, and life is the dose which he tells us to take. You know how, when the doctor orders you a tonic, it comes up labelled: THE MIXTURE, FOR MARY JANE, TO BE TAKEN THREE TIMES A DAY AFTER MEALS. It gives you a sense of pride that the doctor should have invented a special tonic for you, until you find that the other girl in the next dormitory has a medicine tasting just the same which seems to have been made up specially for her. But when we are dealing with Almighty God's prescriptions for us it's not like that; the mixture is made up specially for us, a mixture of pleasant and unpleasant things; no two human lives are ever quite alike. The mixture, for Mary Jane, no one else. Offer that up, with the chalice; all that is going to happen to you, all that is going to become of you; the fun you are going to have, the love which will one day, please God, come into your life, with the rest. And in what spirit is the offering to be made? We are just coming on to that. The priest bows down with his hands on the altar, looking at the host which carries with it the sacrifice of all he is, at the chalice which carries with it the sacrifice of all that is to become of him. And he says: " Lord, let us meet thee with our spirits humbled, in a crushed frame of mind, and by thee be lifted up. So may the sacrifice we offer this day to thee, our Lord and God, be the kind of sacrifice thou desirest." You see, we've been making this offering of our lives to God and feeling pretty generous, rather fine fellows, as we did it; and then suddenly we remember how frightfully unimportant a single human life like that must, in a sense, be to him. When we have been trying to get him interested in our ridiculous little affairs, our wholly unimportant births, marriages and deaths, we feel like a child that has just shown its mother some staring, shapeless picture, some terribly bad poem that didn't rhyme or scan or make sense, and expected her to say, " Very nice, darling ". The Mass is like that all through, you see; we alternate continually between rushing to God with the consciousness of our needs, and then being driven back into a kind of shame-faced, tongue-tied humility by the thought of God's majesty and our insignificance. Those are the two motifs that constantly cross and recross, making up the pattern of the dance for us. Yes, offer him your life by all means; but don't forget your sense of proportion. Don't forget that it's very much the same situation as when you stoop down and pick up a butterfly that has made a forced landing and isn't feeling too good; " Poor thing," you say, and make as if to stroke its wings. That is how we ought to see our lives, if we are to see things in proportion. We lie there humbled and crushed, and God picks us up ; that is the kind of sacrifice he desires.

And then there's the third prayer, to the Holy Spirit,

rather unexpectedly. At least I suppose it is addressed to the Holy Spirit. "Come, Almighty, Eternal God, the Sanctifier, and bless the sacrifice that waits here to do honour to thy holy Name." If I may be a liturgical bore for a moment, let me point out that this is probably our equivalent, in the Latin rite, for what the Greek churches call the Epiclesis, that is, the invocation of the Holy Spirit. In the Greek rites, that invocation is made AFTER the Consecration, and (according to them) it is at that point, not at the moment of Consecration, that the change in the Elements takes place. We, with our Latin habit of mind, don't think of the Holy Spirit as waiting till the last moment and then suddenly interfering to supernaturalize what is being done. No, we like to think of him as patiently at work all the time, from the very minute when we have finished with the Offertory and the sacrifice is lying there ready. You know how, when you are making the fire at a picnic, you want everything to be quite still until you have got your match lit and the first twigs crackling, and then you want a puff of wind, not too strong or sudden, which will gradually spread the flame, go on spreading the flame, till the fire is really going? So it is with this burnt-sacrifice of ours; we want the Holy Spirit to be gently breathing on it from the first moment when it is really ready, kindling our hearts and making them glow, while he kindles our material offerings of bread and wine into a supernatural flame, which is Christ's Body and Blood.

There, I've given you two whole sermons, each of them lasting about a quarter of an hour, discussing the Offertory; and I suppose the Offertory, in the

Mass itself, only takes about three or four minutes. I'm not expecting you to remember all that I've been saying and go through it in your head every time you hear Mass. No, it is enough that your mood, while the Offertory takes place, should chime in with the mood of the dance at that point; three movements, self-oblation, self-obliteration, self-consecration by the invoking of the Holy Spirit.

VIII

LAVABO, SUSCIPE SANCTA TRINITAS

My feet are set on firm ground; where thy people gather, Lord, I will join in blessing thy name. Ps. xxv.

VIII

LAVABO, SUSCIPE SANCTA TRINITAS

My feet are set on firm ground; where thy people gather, Lord, I will join in blessing thy name. Ps. xxv.

WE'VE just got on as far as the incense. I don't think we'll talk about that, because it only comes in sung Mass; and personally I never find it possible to devise any system for attending a sung Mass devoutly all the time; the choir make so much noise that I can't hear myself pray. I thought instead I would give you a few minutes of moral theology. Every Catholic is bound to hear the *whole* of the Mass every Sunday. But how much is the least that is allowed to count, in the sense that if you've heard that much of the 8 you needn't hear the 9?

As we all know, at least I hope we do, the Mass can be divided into three bits, a beginning, an end, and a middle, and you haven't heard Mass *at all* unless you have heard two of those three bits, and one of the two bits you heard was the middle one. The third bit is pretty clearly defined; it is from the ablutions to the end of the Last Gospel. If you have got to cook the breakfast, or are in a hurry for any other legitimate reason, you can go as soon as the priest holds out the chalice towards the server—

or, if there are Communions, as soon as it is clear that the priest has finished his own Communion. But what ordinarily worries us is not the question of leaving too soon. It's a much more debatable point where, exactly, the first break in the Mass comes. The point, I mean, after which you cannot claim to have heard Mass at all, even if you stop on to the very end; it's too late. I have heard it put as early as the beginning of the Gospel; I have heard it put as late as the Sanctus—but that isn't an opinion I would like to stake my chances of going to Heaven on. It always seems to me the safest principle to lay down is this: The dividing line comes at the collection. By that I mean the first collection, not the second, if there are two. Not that the collection is a particularly important incident in the Mass; but it wouldn't be sensible to send the man round with the plate till everybody was there who was going to be there, would it? And because the collection normally starts with the Offertory (when there is somebody different from the server to take it up) I should say that the first of the three bits was down to the Offertory, without bothering very much about whether the Offertory was just beginning or whether they had already got to the incense.

May I say two things about all that? One is, do try and get out of the habit of saying " I was late for Mass one Sunday " when you go to Confession. It may simply mean that you committed a sin of irreverence by turning up in the middle of the Epistle; it may be that you broke the law of the Church by not turning up till the *Ite missa est*. Do try and get into the habit of telling the priest WHAT HAPPENED; nothing is more annoying in the confessional than being told that the penitent has been careless about other people's property, and being expected to understand that he means burning down one or two hay-ricks. In this matter of hearing Mass, it's so much better to say, " One Sunday I only came in to Mass while they were saying the Epistle ", or " the *Ite missa est* ", as the case may be, and then we all know where we are, and no questions are needed.

The other thing is this; don't start out with the intention of being late for Mass, anyhow on days when Mass is of obligation. However boring the sermons are, don't time yourself so as to miss the sermon. Don't deliberately miss part of the Mass; the Mass, as I've been trying to explain, is all one whole thing, one whole action, not just a collection of spare parts. You ought to want to live through it with the priest. And it is a sin of irreverence, for which you are entirely responsible, if you MAKE PLANS for missing part of it. Moreover, you know perfectly well that you *really* know where your hat is, that the buses don't run at the proper intervals on Sunday, and that the church is about two minutes' more walk than you always pretend. Consequently, in your effort to avoid the boring sermon, you are very liable to roll in just as the warning bell rings for the Consecration; and then you come to Confession and ask me, " Please, Father, was that a mortal sin? " If only people would take the trouble to avoid deliberate venial sins, the world would be a much happier place. If you'd started out for Church meaning to be in time, you would have been there for the collection, and you would now be confessing a venial sin of irreverence, if that. Instead of which, here we are wasting our time in the confessional, keeping all the other people waiting, while we try to decide whether it was a mortal sin; whether the conductor slipping in to the Corner house to have a quick one was the sort of accident you could have foreseen or the sort of accident you couldn't have foreseen. Do try to think of the Mass as one single experience which you want to share with the priest. It's not like listening to the news on the wireless, which is all different items, so that you can say " I think we may as well switch it off, now, they've got on to the football results ". It's as if you were to say, " I think I shall read this detective story, but I mean to skip the first two chapters and the last three ". The Mass is a whole.

Well, that's enough about that; let's get on to where the priest washes his hands. I always wonder whether the faithful think the clergy never wash at home, they do so much of it in public. Bishops are at it all the time. I dare say originally it was quite a practical sort of wash, but there's not much point in it now unless the thurifer has been eating butter-scotch in the sacristy and made the chains sticky. But even if it's only a survival, I think it makes an awfully good symbol. Washing your hands gives you the feeling of having finished with the last thing and going on to the next; of having something behind you that's over and done with, something new stretching out before you. I think you get that sense best after a long railway journey, when you've reached the place you are staying at and go up to wash. It isn't merely getting your hands and face clean that gives you a good feeling, even if you have been drawing your initials in the damp on the carriage-window. It brings home to you, somehow, the sense of having arrived; and on the top of that, the sense that there is going to be a meal before long. Now, in the Mass we are trying to put the dust of the world behind us for a bit, and going into a king's presence to share a royal banquet; we shouldn't feel comfortable about that if we hadn't at least made some gesture of preparing ourselves for it. Only a gesture, perhaps—after all, we don't always get *quite* all the ink off our hands before lunch, do we?—but it's better than nothing.

When we were talking about the priest's preparation, I was saying that it ought to make us feel shut off from the wicked world, shut in together in a cosy family party. And at the *Lavabo* I think this feeling ought to return to us, even more strongly. For this reason; in the primitive Church the catechumens, that is, the people who hadn't been baptized yet, but were learning to be Christians, were apprenticed to the job of being Christians, only stayed till half-way through the Mass; after the sermon they were turned out. From the Offertory onwards the Mass was to be entirely a family affair. It's true that under the modern discipline of the Church we don't turn non-Catholics away. But I think the positive side of that feeling ought to be with us still; as the priest goes to wash his hands we ought to be rather stimulated by the sense that this is our show; there is a business-like feeling in the air; if I may use a very indelicate comparison, it's like when somebody is going to fell a tree or something of that kind, and he spits on his hands as he faces up to it. Not that I would ever want any of you to do anything so unladylike; but when the priest washes his hands at Mass we might, I think, be allowed to think (somewhere at the back of our minds) of the workman spitting on his hands as he really gets to work. Once more, as at the Preparation, we say to ourselves, "Now we're off". Let's just have a look at what the psalm says.

"With the pure in heart I will wash my hands clean, and take my place among them at the altar, listening there to the sound of thy praises, telling the story of all thy wonderful deeds. How well, Lord, I love thy house in its beauty, the place where thy own glory dwells! Lord, never count this soul lost with the wicked, this life among the bloodthirsty; hands ever stained with guilt, palms ever itching for a bribe! Be it mine to guide my steps clear of wrong; deliver me in thy mercy. My feet are set on firm ground; where thy people gather, Lord, I will join in blessing thy name."

When I was talking to you, only you've forgotten about it by now, about the psalm *Judica* at the beginning of Mass, I was saying that some people think the situation there is that of some Levite who has been exiled from his country on a false charge, but now has been acquitted; and the psalm represents the joy he feels at being allowed to go back to the altar of God again. Curiously, I feel it in my bones—I may be quite wrong—that in this psalm too the situation is that of a man who has been falsely accused, and then acquitted. I think he had been accused of taking a bribe, either to give a false judgement or else to give false evidence in a law-court; there had been a murder trial, and it was thought that the murderers had bribed him to take their side. Then, somehow, it is all cleared up, and he can shew his face again. Do you see how much more point that gives to the whole thing; " Lord, never count *my* soul lost with the wicked, this life among the bloodthirsty, hands ever stained with guilt, palms ever itching for a bribe." It's all right now, his character is re-established; he will wash his hands with the pure in heart—they will no longer shrink from him, as if they expected to see blood in the basin—and then take his place among them as they form a semi-circle round the altar. The old translation says, " I will compass thy altar, O Lord ", which, of course, is nonsense; there was no mulberry-bush business about the Jewish altars any more than about ours, you didn't go round and round them. No, the author of the psalm is going to be one of the ring of worshippers that stands round the altar; he won't be ashamed any longer to be seen doing it.

Well, I don't suppose most of you have had the experience of being wrongly suspected of doing things you hadn't done; probably rather the other way. You may have been told you were talking in the dormitory when you were really only humming, but I don't suppose you've known what it was to be in real disgrace, and then to be proved innocent after all. But you can imagine something of the thrill of it. And I think we, at this point in the Mass, ought to feel something of the same thrill, not about being innocent and proved innocent, but about having been guilty and now being forgiven. We are so constantly told, aren't we, to go on and on about our sins, weeping over them and never forgetting them; I wonder if we don't need more encouragement to rejoice, to feel really bucked, that our sins have been forgiven? And yet we know that they *have* been forgiven, through the merits of Jesus Christ. Don't you think, when we see the priest washing his hands and preparing to take his place among the clean of heart, we ought to try and realize how forgiven our sins are, how utterly put behind us, washed away like the dust of railway-travel?

And then the priest, who has been marching to and fro and turning round and bowing to the altar in a rather pleased, forgiven sort of way, comes to a halt again in the middle and bends down to say that nice, comprehensive prayer, the *Suscipe sancta Trinitas*. Once more, as at the beginning of Mass, he can't remind himself that we are a family party, shut out from our sins and from all the noise and dust of the world, without reminding himself that we unite, in offering the Mass, not only with all faithful Christians all over the world, but with the dead too. And especially those glorious dead, the saints, who are worshipping God at his heavenly altars as we at his earthly. So he bends down and asks the holy Trinity to receive this sacrifice of ours; we are offering it primarily to commemorate our Lord's Passion, Resurrection and Ascension, that trinity of mysteries round which the Mass revolves. But at the same time we are doing honour to the blessed saints, Blessed Mary ever-Virgin, St. John the Baptist, the holy apostles Peter and Paul, them and all the saints, all the lot of them. Their salvation is assured now, so we offer it for our salvation and in their honour; we would like them to remember us in their prayers at the throne of grace, as we, here, remember them with thanksgiving. With these, the pure in heart, we will form one single ring about the eternal altar.

IX

SECRET PRAYERS, PREFACE

I will praise thee with the angels for company, bowed low before thy holy temple. Ps. cxxxvii.

IX

SECRET PRAYERS, PREFACE

I will praise thee with the angels for company, bowed low before thy holy temple.   Ps. cxxxvii.

WE HAVE just got to the Secret prayers. Why is it that the priest says a lot of the Mass under his breath, instead of shouting out the Latin for everybody to hear? Even in a learned institution like this, where some of you have probably got on to the third conjugation. Honestly I don't know. Roughly speaking, I think it's true to say that the priest at Low Mass says aloud all the parts that are sung at a High Mass, and murmurs the rest. Roughly speaking, at a High Mass the priest only murmurs when the choir shouts. But which way about was it? Did the priest say to himself, " I can't be bothered to say this bit out loud, with those sopranos howling me down all the time "? Or did the organist say, " The holy priest doesn't seem to have much to say for himself just now; come on, boys, let 'em have it "? I don't know. I only know I always rather wish these Secret prayers after the Offertory were said out loud, because they are so very attractive, some of them. Take the one for last Sunday: " This sacrifice, Lord, we bring, to win thy favour; bring our sins, for thy mercy to pardon, bring our wavering hearts, for thee to point them to their goal "—don't tell me that isn't a jolly prayer. Or take the one on the eve of Passion Sunday:

" Lord, we beseech thee, accept these offerings, and restore us to thy favour, subduing, with merciful violence, even rebel wills like ours "— don't tell me that isn't a jolly prayer. But I've got to mumble them.

However, there's one good thing about it; it's a trap for the unwary; it catches you out if you weren't attending. I don't mean that holy Church put the Secret prayers in for that reason; holy Church wouldn't be as unsporting as that. No, it's just a lucky accident that they come here. You see, it's just half-way through the Mass, and we aren't all of us very good at keeping our attention fixed for more than a quarter of an hour. And some of us are sleepy; of course, you had a rotten night, with the girl in the next bed talking in her sleep like that. And even if you aren't actually in danger of dozing off, your attention has perhaps begun to wander; why does that girl in front of you wear plaits when they obviously don't suit her? and so on and so on *per omnia saecula saeculorum*! Ah, you weren't expecting that! You thought I was going on mumbling to myself. Even the server was caught napping really; he only said " Amen " because he couldn't think of anything else to say. Well, *Dominus vobiscum*; are you all with me now? *Et cum spiritu tuo*; good, that's all right. Then, *Sursum corda*; lift up your hearts. That doesn't mean that you are to concentrate your attention on a particular valve somewhere inside your chest, and imagine yourself as heaving it up into the air. God isn't just up in the air; he's everywhere. It means take a deep breath and let your whole self go OUT to God. In what spirit? Penitence? No. Confidence? No. Adoration? No; but you're getting warmer. Love?

Not exactly. No—gratitude; Let us give *thanks* to our Lord God. All the other things too, of course, are perfectly in place; but the characteristic attitude of the Christian people in worshipping their God is thankfulness. That is why we call it the Holy Eucharist. First and foremost, the Mass means reminding ourselves of our Redemption—Jesus Christ was crucified for me. First and foremost, then, we are catching our breath at a great deliverance, and thanking God for it.

That's what I tell you when I say *Gratias agamus Domino Deo nostro*, and you agree with me; *Dignum et justum est*, you say, " By all means; obviously it's the right and proper thing to do ". How disconcerting it is, now and again, to come across people who pick up your words and examine them, and turn them inside out! You know the sort of thing I mean; when an old lady says to you, " I'm very sorry to hear your mamma has broken her leg ", and you say, " Yes, it is rather a bore for her, isn't it? " And then the old lady really gets going: " My dear, when you've broken your leg you will realize that it's a great deal worse than boring; it's an extremely painful and dangerous accident. Of course I know that your dear mother is a very energetic woman, and I expect she finds the time hang heavy on her hands, which I suppose is what you mean by *a bore*. But I hope you will realize that she is having a very painful time, and the less shrieking and jumping there is in the passages, the sooner she will get well ". Of course you know all that, and you long to say something you're too polite to say, and the incident has to be regarded as closed. I think the priest is a tiny bit like that when you say *Dignum et justum est*, right and proper. He goes on mumbling away, "*Dignum et justum est*, right and proper, I should think it WAS right and proper". (You mustn't mind; we priests get like that.)

Dignum est; it is worthy of our dignity as human beings, *justum est*, it is suited to our position as creatures, *aequum est*, it is only fair, since we are reprieved criminals, that we should always be giving thanks wherever we are. And there is a fourth word he uses, *salutare*; what does that mean?

I don't know what translation they give you in your book; probably "conducive to salvation", or something of that sort. But I don't think that's the idea, I think the meaning is, "It's a healthy sign". It's a healthy sign when a Christian finds himself, at all sorts of odd times and in all sorts of queer places, wanting to thank God. You know the sort of thing a doctor will call a healthy sign if he is talking about the condition of your body; a good appetite, for example—if he's told that you got outside a couple of pancakes, when you're supposed to have measles, he says that is a healthy sign. And that's the great thing about gratitude in the Christian soul; it may not be very important in itself, but it's a healthy sign. The person who is continually grousing and nursing grievances may be all right; our temperaments and even our digestions have a good deal to do with it; you can't tell. But if a person is the other way, is always grateful to God for the small mercies and the things that do go right, I think that is a good indication that he or she is on the road to heaven.

That business about being grateful to God always, all the time, is of course leading up to the next fact which calls for our attention; the Preface isn't the same all the year round. At the different seasons of the year we commemorate the different stages by which our Lord Jesus Christ achieved our redemption. And at each of those seasons, we give a fresh twist to the great chant of thankfulness which we call the Preface. At all times and in all places we ought to be giving you thanks, Almighty God, but it does so happen that this particular time—Christmas or Easter or Pentecost, or whatever it may be—is one at which the gratitude we feel ought to be something quite exceptional, something quite out of the common. This was the time when you became a little Baby at Bethlehem; how grateful we ought to be! This was the time when you conquered death for us; how grateful we ought to be! This was the time when you sent the Holy Spirit to cheer us up on our lonely march through the world without you; how grateful we ought to be! Grateful always, of course, but more grateful than ever just now.

Why those Prefaces are so good, I don't quite know. They are not frightfully good or frightfully clear Latin, but they manage to get in a lot, somehow, in a small space. At Christmas, we have to be specially grateful, because a new light has flashed across the world, a lightning-flash in which we saw God made visible, at Bethlehem, and ever since our eyes are home-sick for the things we cannot see. At the Epiphany, we have to be specially grateful, because this sight of God made mortal is a kind of beacon-star which heralds the dawn of our own immortality. In Passion-tide, we have to be specially grateful, because, on Calvary, Jesus Christ beat Satan with his own weapons; found him wielding, like a club, the tree of Paradise which was the cause of Adam's undoing, and knocked him out with another tree, the

Tree of the Cross. In Easter-tide, we have to be specially grateful, at this season when Christ himself is offered for us as our paschal Lamb, who by his blood shed for us has destroyed the sentence of death passed against us. At the Ascension, we have to be specially grateful, because, after rising again, he ascended visibly into Heaven, so that the reunion of his Manhood with the eternal Being of God might make us all divine. At Pentecost, we have to be specially grateful, because now that he sits at God's right hand, he has sent the Holy Spirit on us, his adopted children, and made the whole world thrill with that gracious influence. Strange, primitive phrases, not in the least the well-worn language of our theological copybooks; they take us back to a time when—dare we say it? theology was somehow richer because it wasn't all so terribly precise.

Even Lent has a Preface of its own, although we don't ordinarily think of Lent as something we ought to be grateful for; we always connect it with not eating sweets or something of that kind. But even in Lent we ought to be specially grateful for this opportunity of chastening our bodies, and so lending wings to our souls; of obtaining, through the observance of it, fresh strength for our struggle on earth, fresh joys of retrospect in Heaven, when it is all over. It's almost a pity, I think, that for so large a part of the year we just have to be content with two Prefaces; a common or garden Preface for week-days, and a longer one on Sundays in honour of the Blessed Trinity. There used, I fancy, to be a lot more variety. I have used a Dominican missal before now in a Dominican Church, and my impression was that in their rite—which, as I told you, has more of the Middle Ages surviving in it than ours—they had a fresh Preface for nearly every day.

After those variations, the Preface always comes round to the same point; it always invites us to think about the blessed choirs of Angels round God's throne, and to unite our praise with theirs. I like to think of it, as I told you once before, as a sort of gradual upward progress first through one rank, then through another, of celestial beings, till at last we reach the throne itself. When you are going home for the holidays, I bet some of you look out of the carriage windows and read the names of the stations to see how near you are getting to London: "Burnham, Bucks—good, we're nearly at Slough; West Drayton and Yiewsley, that's the stuff; look, there's the Underground beginning, that means Ealing Broadway; here's Hanwell, that's the asylum, over on the right"—and then the delicious slowing-down into the platform at Paddington. Well, it's like that, or ought to be, when we say the Preface. Here are the Angels, but we must get beyond the Angels; here are the Dominations, but we want to get to the real Ruler of the world; here are the Authorities, but we must get to the source of all authority; here are the Powers of Heaven, but we want something stronger still; here are the Seraphim, so happy in their love, but their love is only a faint glow compared with that Divine Furnace of love which kindles them. Yes, we are glad to see them, and wave to them all, but we can't stop; we want to get right into the middle of things, right up to God's throne. Their cries of adoration ring louder and louder as we go; and we join in as best we can with our ridiculous little squeaky trebles—they won't mind, and God won't mind. *Supplici confessione dicentes*—and then, like the engine suddenly shutting off steam just beyond Royal Oak, the priest bends down and drops his voice to a low murmur: *Sanctus, sanctus, sanctus, Dominus Deus Sabaoth.*

If you are musical, and compose Masses when you grow up, don't encourage the choir to make the *Sanctus* into a great hullabaloo, as some of them do; it's all wrong. There's nothing more splendid in the Mass than that bowing of the head, that dropping of the voice, when the priest gets to this point. It's like walking in a terrible blustering wind and then suddenly turning a corner and finding yourself under the lee of some great rock, in absolute stillness. The whole dance of the Mass depends, just here, on getting that effect of sudden calm, sudden dying-away of noise. The priest has been standing bolt upright, arms extended, talking in a loud voice as if he was shouting How-d'ye-do's to all the ranks of the celestial hierarchy as he shoots past them; and then quite suddenly the movement is reversed. He bends down, he talks in a murmur. Why? Thinking of his sins? No, not this time. In humility? No, not in humility this time. Not even out of reverence, quite. He bends down, now that he has reached the very door of the heavenly temple, and takes one look through the keyhole. And he says " SSSH! I've seen it! The glory of God, that fills earth and Heaven, shining in front of me. Take off your shoes, and let's go in very quietly, on tip-toe, quite close. Don't pay any more attention to those Angels and Dominations and people; come up here and take a look. There, do you see? Take off your shoes, all of you, and let's go in very quietly, on tip-toe."

X

SANCTUS, TE IGITUR, COMMEMORATION OF THE LIVING

This first of all I ask, that petition, prayer, entreaty and thanksgiving should be offered for all mankind. 1 *Tim. ii.* 1.

X

SANCTUS, TE IGITUR, COMMEMORATION OF THE LIVING

This first of all I ask, that petition, prayer, entreaty and thanksgiving should be offered for all mankind. I *Tim. ii.* I.

IN MY last sermon, I hadn't time to talk about one feature which had just come into the Mass for the first time; I mean the bell. Why do we ring bells such a lot? I suspect that the little tinkly bell in the sanctuary is only a sort of midget edition of the big bell or bells up in the Church tower. Just as, at the Introit, the priest says only one verse of a psalm when he ought to be saying the whole psalm through, so, I suspect, the bells in the tower were meant to be rung a lot more than they are, only the sacristan was too idle to hang on to a great rope every time the priest got to the *Sanctus*. You see, it would be jolly for sick people if they could follow the Mass all the way through, instead of only hearing the Consecration bell rung at the High Mass on Sundays. I may be quite wrong about all this; I'm only making it up. I could talk to you for hours and hours about Church bells. Why are they christened, for example, like human beings? I don't mean they get the grace of faith, but there is a kind of christening ceremony, and they are given names. That's surely odd; nothing else in church gets a name given to it. You would think it very unusual if I started calling the alms-dish Percy. I suppose bells are so much mixed up with the important events of our lives; the wedding peals and the funeral chimes and so on, that the medieval people used to have a kind of friendly feeling for them; they were the public pets of the village. They were also supposed to drive the devil away, and I must say I know a lot of Church bells that would drive me away if I were the devil. But we really haven't time to talk about all that; let's confine our attention to the little tinkly bell.

Our attention—it says in the books that the bell is rung at Mass to excite the attention and devotion of the faithful. It seems to me a very queer notion that at High Mass anyhow, when the priest has been singing his way so vigorously through the Preface, and the choir has just started with great chords on the organ to get through the *Sanctus*, a tiny little bell in the sanctuary should have the effect of waking the faithful up. I should have thought that kind of faithful would have needed a siren. No, honestly I think it's all part of this business about the holy Angels, and the priest feeling that he's just arrived at the door of Heaven and can look through the key-hole. Having arrived at the door, we ring the bell. And we don't do it to amuse ourselves; we do it to show the holy Angels that we are there. "Please say that Mary Jane has come to call"—that is the point of the Sanctus-bell. Or, if you like to keep up that allegory of the train getting into Paddington which we were talking about last Sunday, you may think of the Sanctus-bell as one of those little tinkly noises that are always going on inside thc signal box when you are waiting for your train at a station. It's supposed to mean, I think, that the line is clear; the next train can come along without any fear of an accident. So, if you prefer to put it that way, say the Sanctus-bell means the line is clear, and Mary Jane can go forging ahead.

Meanwhile, the priest has gone silent again. As I say, that may be simply because at High Mass the choir haven't nearly got to the end of the *Sanctus*, and the priest doesn't wait till they do. At Low Mass, it's a good effective silence, don't you think, when the Canon of the Mass begins? A clean, crisp sort of silence which gives you the impression that something rather important is happening; everybody is holding their breaths in excitement. And, of course, if you are the sort of person who prefers to say your own prayers instead of following the liturgy, it's a useful silence too. It's the time you ought to be praying for all the people you want to pray for; and a great many other people as well, hungry Germans and persecuted Poles and atheists in Russia and atheists in our own country. But these sermons are meant for people who do like to follow the liturgy; so we must take a peep over the priest's shoulder and see what it is he's reading about. We have got it in our own books, with a crib; the crib starts " Thee therefore, O most clement Father ", which doesn't sound much like English. What is he really saying?

It is as though he had just remembered that he hasn't done anything at all about the bread and wine since the Offertory; they might just as well not have been there, all this time. So he gets back to work, to the real sacrifice. The liturgical people make a great deal of fuss about the word " therefore ", but there's no need to. You will find in the Latin dictionary that *Igitur* means " therefore ", but it's a very weak word really, it's hardly more than clearing your throat: " Chrrrm! Well then, as I was saying "—that's all it means. And the priest says, " Well then, we know what a loving Father you are—the Preface has told us all about that; and we are coming to you *Per Jesum Christum Dominum nostrum*, because our Lord Jesus Christ said we might, and he would make it all right for us. And we want you to accept from us, and to bless so that they will be supremely useful to us, these gifts of ours, these offerings of ours, this holy sacrifice, so virgin-pure." He talks in that exaggerated way about a round piece of unleavened bread that has come out of a tin, and a small quantity of not frightfully good wine from Australia because, as I say, the action of the Mass is all one, and time doesn't count. The bread and wine have not yet been consecrated; but they are going to be consecrated so soon that it is all one as if they were; he is already making to Almighty God the eternal sacrifice of Calvary.

And then he goes on to describe who it is he is making this offering for. Don't let's forget the meaning of that; every grace you and I ever get is given to us only because Jesus Christ died for us and was offered up instead of us, bore our punishment instead of us. And in the Mass, which is a continuation of Calvary, we are, as it were, trying to push our Lord forward and make him the representative of all the people we want to pray for. You know how, if a crowd of you have to make some rather embarrassing request from some rather important person—if Reverend Mother comes down, and you want to ask her for a holiday, you all stand there trying to push one another forward? " No, go on, *you* say it . . . No, don't be so silly, she wouldn't pay any attention to me, *you* say it ", and so on. Well, in a way that's what we are doing in this part of the Mass. We want God to do something about all the unhappy people in Europe who have nowhere to go, nowhere to live, and so we put forward at the head of them our Lord Jesus Christ, who had nowhere to lay his head—surely Almighty God will pay attention now? And so on. That's what offering our Lord in the Mass means—piling all our needs on to his shoulders, his patient shoulders; hiding all our defects behind his robe, his big, comfortable robe.

So we start, you see, by praying for the whole Catholic Church. Not just for us; we are only a fragment of the Catholic Church. And there is only one altar really; that altar behind me is the same thing as the High Altar at St. Peter's and the High Altar at Westminster Cathedral, and the nasty little soap-box on which, perhaps, some miserable, exiled priest is saying Mass as best he can, somewhere out in Siberia. Only one altar, and the whole Catholic Church is one congregation, worshipping together; all of you as you kneel at Mass here are only specimens, good specimens, let's hope, of the whole Catholic Church which is kneeling in this chapel, only you can't see it. Just as the Mass cuts out time, it cuts out space. Shove up a bit closer there, and make room for those Esquimaux . . .

But of course this terrific thing, the unity of the

Christian Church, isn't an easy thing for our imaginations to grasp. Most of us find it easier to get excited over a person than over an institution. Our patriotism is more easily excited by " God Save the King " than by " Rule Britannia "; because King George, even if we haven't seen him, is a voice on the wireless, whereas Britannia is only an imaginary female on the back of a coin. So in the Mass we focus the whole idea of the Catholic Church for ourselves by seeing it as represented in one man, Pope Pius XII. We ask God to give the Church peace, that is, a let-up from all its persecutions; to give it unity, that is, more friendliness among its existing members and better hopes of bringing back strayed Christians into its fold; and to give it wise government. And all those ideas are easily summed up for us when we think about the Holy Father at Rome, and think about what he is thinking about. But at the same time we are not meant to forget that we have got special ties, special loyalties of our own. So, after mentioning Pope Pius XII as a person we want specially blessed, please, we go on to explain to Almighty God that we belong to the Shrewsbury diocese; you know, Bishop Moriarty.

In the Missal I use, I don't know about yours, the Pope's name isn't there, and the Bishop's name isn't there; instead of putting in Pius and the Bishop's name the Missal says our Pope N. and our Bishop N. The point of that, of course, is that popes aren't immortal and bishops aren't immortal; they are only spare parts which can be replaced. And from the priest's point of view that comes in particularly well just here—you see, it puts him in his place. If he was tempted to feel at all self-conceited over the honour which is done him when he is allowed to offer this tremendous sacrifice, he is pulled up now by the thought that he, like the Pope and the Bishop, is only a spare part which can be replaced. The Mass is offered in this chapel not by Monsignor Knox but by *your priest* N. N. stands for anybody; any other priest would do just as well. Hundreds of thousands of Masses are being said all over the world, and this is just one of them. You know how they put down little reflectors of red glass at the corner of the road where there is a cross-roads, or where some sharp turn makes it dangerous; and as your car comes up at night, the light of the headlamps is caught by these and reflected back? Well, the priest ought to think of himself as one little piece of red glass; the moment when he consecrates, when he offers sacrifice, is the moment in which the prayer of the universal Church is caught up and reflected in him. Only for a moment; then he goes back to being a dull, ordinary piece of glass again.

Having been through that bit of self-humiliation, the priest is now allowed to remember that he is a human being, and some people do interest him more than others. He is allowed, for a moment, to stop talking Latin; to think, for a moment, of the people for whose needs he personally wants this Mass to be an availing sacrifice. I ask God to convert Stalin or whatever it may be. And immediately after that I go on to say *et omnium circumstantium*: "Please don't think I want you to listen to *me* more than to any of those horrible little creatures who are fidgeting behind me. *Quorum tibi fides cognita est, et nota devotio*—they do really believe in you, they are really quite pious, some of them, and each of them has her own intention that she's thinking about at this moment, and it's just as good as mine. So please take it that this goes for Mary Jane's intention as well as mine. *Pro quibus tibi offerimus;* I am offering this sacrifice for them, just as much as for myself. *Vel qui tibi offerunt*, and they, just as much as myself, are *offering* this Mass, so please don't convert Stalin if you would sooner convert Mary Jane's aunt. They are offering the Mass *pro se suisque omnibus*, for themselves and all they love; their souls want saving, they need health of body and soul, preservation of body and soul from all harm that might befall them; some of them asked rather specially to be called this morning, so please bless every one of them every bit as much as me."

I'm afraid we are making very slow time, and I would have liked to talk about the *Communicantes* this afternoon, but that's too big a subject and too fresh a subject to tackle now. What I want to get firmly into your heads now is this—that when you see me standing up there mumbling to myself and apparently taking no notice of you, all dressed up in silk like a great pin-cushion, you mustn't think of me as something quite apart, at a distance from you, uninterested in your feelings and your concerns. On the contrary, I am standing there like a great pin-cushion for you to stick pins into me—all the things you want to pray about, all the things you want for yourself and all the worries that are going on at home, are part of the prayer that I am saying, and I couldn't prevent them being part of my intentions in saying the Mass, even if I wanted to.

XI

COMMUNICANTES, CONSECRATION

Thy life shall be as it were hanging before thee. Deut. xxviii.

XI

COMMUNICANTES, CONSECRATION

Thy life shall be as it were hanging before thee. Deut. xxviii.

LAST time, I'm afraid, we left off in the middle of a sentence. The bit of the Mass we are coming to now begins with a participle, *Communicantes*, and the sentence goes on for rather over twenty lines without any main verb in it. And I am sure that any of you who do Latin have been told that you must never write a sentence without a main verb in it. Some clever people think this participle, *Communicantes*, is just hanging in the air; like when you send a person a Christmas card which just says WISHING YOU A HAPPY CHRISTMAS—there is no main verb in that; or when you end your letter home, " hoping this finds you as it leaves me "—there is no main verb in that. But I don't believe that's so here. I think the participle agrees with the last set of people who have been mentioned; and that is YOU. In coming to Mass, in offering your intentions at Mass, you are uniting yourselves with the great string of saints which follows. *Et memoriam venerantes*—uniting yourselves in a rather distant, apologetic way, making a kind of mental curtsey to our Blessed Lady and St. Peter and all the rest of them. But you do, nevertheless, unite yourself in thought with this string of saints; you take your place, as it were, at the end of the queue. We have already reminded ourselves that the Mass is all one, and that all Christians hearing Mass in all parts of the world are present in chapel when we have Mass here. But now we see that the thing goes wider than that; the Saints in heaven, too, from our Lady downwards are part of it all; you, as a faithful Christian, are holding hands with the next person, so to speak, and she with the next person, and so on and on and back and back and up and up till you get to our Blessed Lady herself.

I don't think we need worry if we don't know all about the saints whose names appear on the list; when we have finished the apostles we go on to the early popes and the early martyrs who suffered at Rome. But, of course, they are only specimens; it's like when you are doing an exam, and you finish up the last question with a scrawl that says NO TIME FOR MORE; either because you hadn't time for any more or because you don't know anything else to say in answer to that particular question. St. Pius V cut down the list, as he cut down everything else in the Mass; "No time for more" seems to have been his motto. But they are all meant to be there really, all your favourite saints, and you are quite right to think of them if you care to, instead of people like St. Cornelius and St. Chrysogonus, who were very holy men, but don't somehow ring a bell.

The server *does* ring a bell at this point. If I have blown my nose or made any other unexpected gesture with my hands since the *Sanctus*, he has probably rung it already by mistake, but this is the place where it is supposed to come, just after the list of saints, when I hold my hands extended over the chalice like *that*. The bell, this time, is really meant to wake you up, unless you want a dig in the back from Mother Clare; it wouldn't do to leave you snoozling on till the actual moment of Consecration—you have got to be ready for it when it comes. And the gesture I make, together with the signs of the Cross which I make immediately afterwards, are a kind of blessing, rather like the blessing I give you when you are going away for the holidays. I give it at Mass to the bread and wine, when they are just going off on a journey, the strangest journey imaginable. They are going to transcend the order of nature altogether. Meanwhile, I ask Almighty God to accept this offering, made on our behalf but also on behalf of his whole family; we never get away from that point, you see—the Mass is all one. I ask that the bread and wine may be blessed; that they may be set apart; that God's promise in connexion with them shall be ratified, that is, shall be kept; that they shall form a reasonable sacrifice, and therefore an acceptable sacrifice. We do not, under the Christian dispensation, offer to God dumb animals or lifeless things, but it will be all right about the bread and wine, because, once consecrated, they will be built into the human Body of our Lord Jesus Christ. And finally, I ask that they may be accepted. Then, with two more signs of the Cross, I ask God to perform this miracle of Transubstantiation.

What happens if the priest falls down dead at this point?

The answer to that is that you say one Hail Mary for my soul and go back to breakfast; there is nothing special that needs to be done about it; I mean about the Mass. For all intents and purposes it hasn't started yet. Three minutes later, when the Consecration has happened, if the priest who is celebrating the Mass falls dead or is taken gravely ill, any other priest who can be got hold of must finish off the Mass, even if he isn't fasting; even if he is under ecclesiastical discipline and is forbidden in the ordinary way to celebrate any Sacrament at all. There are a lot of exciting rubrics like that at the beginning of the big Latin Missal, which aren't printed in the book you use. I only mention the circumstance here so as to ram home the fact that the really important moment of the Mass has now arrived. True, the Mass is all one; true, all the bits we have been talking about in the last few sermons I've given you are really part of the sacrifice. But if the Consecration doesn't happen, all that goes for nothing; it's like the burnt faggots that lie about in the grate when the coal has never lit. It is only with the Consecration that the sacrifice of the Mass is achieved.

I have represented the Mass to you, more than once, as a kind of ritual dance. And here, at this most solemn part of it, I think you can say with all reverence that it becomes a kind of ritual drama. The priest finds himself, almost absent-mindedly, *acting the part* of Jesus Christ. In consecrating, he recalls the history of Maundy Thursday evening; just in a few sentences which include the actual words in which the Sacrament was instituted. But he is not content merely to tell the story; he acts it; he suits the action to the word.

When he says the words " he took bread " or " he took the cup ", the priest suits the action to the word. So, too, at the words, " lifting up his eyes to Heaven " the priest lifts up his own eyes to Heaven. That is a curious point; none of the Gospels mention that our Lord did that; St. Paul in the Corinthians doesn't mention that our Lord did that. Was it just a guess? Or has the rite of the Roman Mass preserved, by a tradition that has lasted nineteen centuries and more, a detail which the sacred authors omitted to mention? I don't know; we shall never know. But that is a digression. What I am trying to explain to you is that the priest does, here, act a part, and the part of our Blessed Lord himself. Isn't that, perhaps, rather an irreverent idea? Why, no; because this isn't ordinary acting, like the plays you act here. When you act, you pretend that somebody is there who isn't there, King Henry the Eighth or Macbeth or somebody. But the priest, in this interval of drama, doesn't pretend that somebody is there who isn't there. Jesus Christ is really there; there's no pretending about it. He is really there, not merely in the sacred Host, but also in the person of the priest. We mustn't say that the priest is Jesus Christ; that would be blasphemy and nonsense. No, but the priest has become a kind of dummy through which, here and now, Jesus Christ is consecrating the Sacrament, just as he did, but in his own person, nineteen hundred years ago.

The most obvious symbol of that is the fact that, between the Consecration and the ablutions, the priest keeps the thumb and first finger of either hand pressed close together, except when he is actually holding the sacred Host between them. The practical purpose of that is obvious; there may be some tiny crumb of the Host sticking to his fingers, and there must be no danger of its dropping. But, as I say, it seems to me the thing is an excellent symbol; a symbol of the fact that the priest, when he consecrates, is turning himself into a kind of slave, a kind of tool; he is abandoning the use of his bodily muscles and lending them to Jesus Christ; he is turning himself into a kind of dummy for Jesus Christ to use exactly as he wants to. You probably couldn't turn a key in the door by taking it between your first finger and your middle finger; at least, you would do it clumsily. I could, because that is the way every priest turns the key of the tabernacle when he gives Communion during Mass; he can't separate his thumb and first finger. I say he can't; I mean he mustn't; but the habit so grows upon you, if you're a priest, that you feel as if it was impossible to separate them; they've got stuck like that, as your mother told you that your face would get stuck if the wind changed while you were making faces.

I've been labouring that point about the priest identifying himself with Jesus Christ in the Mass because that is the thing you ought to be doing, first and foremost, while the Consecration is happening; you want to identify yourself with Jesus Christ, with Jesus Christ being offered there in the sacred Host.

What you come to Mass for isn't to worship Jesus Christ present in the Sacrament of the altar; that isn't Mass, that's Benediction. You come to Mass to offer Jesus Christ with the priest, and to offer yourself to God with Jesus Christ and as a part of Jesus Christ. Of course it's true that at the actual moment when the priest elevates you are taught to look up and say, " My Lord and my God "; look up again when he elevates the chalice, though I have never found any book which gave you any prayer to say when the priest elevates the Chalice. But that is just politeness; obviously you couldn't allow our Blessed Lord to become specially present, close at your side, without saying " How do you do? " to him; but that is not what you came to Mass for. You came to Mass to offer him to God, and yourself with him.

Possibly you will complain that you have heard a lot about this before; long ago, when we were talking about the Offertory, I was saying that when we give the priest bread and wine to perform the sacrifice with, we are really meant to be presenting ourselves, our souls and bodies, as a living sacrifice to God. Yes, I know, but that act of oblation you were making earlier on in the Mass was only a kind of rehearsal for the great act of oblation which you ought to be making now. A kind of rehearsal. I'm not sure that isn't rather a good way of putting it. Most of you are rather mad on acting, so you'll understand what I mean when I say that there is all the difference in the world between rehearsing your lines, even at a dress rehearsal, and having to speak them on the night. The footlights and the audience, somehow, make all the difference. Really, of course, if you break down and make a fool of yourself it will be a great relief and delight to the audience; it will make their day for them. But that side of the picture doesn't present itself to your mind, does it, when you actually step into the glare of the footlights. You have ceased to be just yourself, and have become a part of the cast; you throw yourself into the thing instinctively, not bothering in the least about the audience and whether they are enjoying themselves. Well, there's the same sort of difference between the Offertory at Mass and the Consecration at Mass; one's the rehearsal, the other's the real thing.

So I would say, don't make too much of that glance which you give when the Host is elevated, and of the prayer which goes with it;-let it be only a momentary burst of recognition. Then relax the effort of your mind, and let yourself be carried away on the stream of intercession which is going on all round you when Jesus Christ is there. Don't get worked up about whether you are praying well or not, just stand down and let our Lord do the praying for you. He has taken over our sacrifice, and he is going to offer it for us.

At this point above all in the Mass, don't bother to try to follow in a book if you find your prayers come easier without. But if you should be following in the book, you will see that the next bit which comes after the Consecration says just what we should want to say. Priest and people (the priest is careful, once more, to associate the whole of the congregation with him, it is their sacrifice, not his)—priest and people remind themselves of our Lord's Passion, Resurrection and Ascension. The last three events of his life; and this new meeting with him reminds us of them all. The Christ who left us at the Ascension has come back to us; the Christ who triumphed over matter by rising from the dead comes back to us under the forms of lifeless things, bread and wine; the Christ who offered himself for us through suffering is impassible now, but offers himself still. With all this in mind, we present to God the oblation we are making to him out of his own gifts to us; his own gifts of bread and wine —but what a change has come over them! Bread, that was meant to sustain our bodies just for a few hours, now ready to bring us eternal life; wine, that might be used to cheer us up just for an evening, now implanting unfailing health in our souls! God's gifts, but so far beyond our ordinary human reach that we are ashamed to accept them; we offer to give them back to him. " No, really, Lord, it's awfully good of you, but we've no right to such gifts as these; please take them back! " We must offer to give them back, offer to share them with him, before we can reconcile ourselves to the idea of actually consuming them, the Body and Blood of Jesus Christ.

XII

PRAYERS OF OFFERING, COMMEMORATION OF THE DEAD

He sits for ever at the right hand of God, offering for our sins a sacrifice that can never be repeated. Heb. x.

XII

PRAYERS OF OFFERING, COMMEMORATION OF THE DEAD

He sits for ever at the right hand of God, offering for our sins a sacrifice that can never be repeated. Heb. x.

THE priest now asks Almighty God to look on the sacrifice which is being made to him "with an indulgent smile".

When we say our prayers, we sound as if we were talking nonsense nearly all the time. I mean, we are using words not in a literal but in a metaphorical sense. And if you complain that "metaphorical" is a long word and you are not quite sure what it means, I can only refer you to the story Abbot Hunter Blair used to tell, of the Scots minister who explained to the congregation in the course of his sermon that he was their shepherd; and then, bending over the pulpit and pointing at the precentor who sat below he said, "I'm your shepherd, and yon's ma wee doggie". Whereupon the precentor looked round and up at him and said, "I'm thenkin' I'm no your wee doggie". So the minister bent over again and said, "Hoots, mon, I was only speakin' metaphoarical". Well, we are always speaking metaphorical; we talk about God as if he was up in the air, when we mean that he is infinitely greater than ourselves, wholly inaccessible by any human means. We talk about our Lord as sitting at his right hand, when all we mean is that he enjoys that close proximity to him, that high place in his favour, which belongs to the favourite of some earthly king who has the privilege of sitting on the right hand of the throne. And so here, when we talk of God smiling we don't mean that he really has a face, really smiles. We only mean that we want him to accept our sacrifice with the same considerate love with which an earthly father would receive a present, and smile indulgently in doing it.

But then; we are inclined to ask why there's any need to offer such a prayer. How could God refuse the sacrifice of his own Son? And why should an indulgent smile be necessary, as if there was something rather inadequate, even something rather imperfect, about this tremendous gift? Well, in order to understand that, I think you want to read on. We ask him to look favourably on this sacrifice and to accept it, just as long ago he accepted the sacrifice of Abel, and the sacrifice of Abraham, and the sacrifice of Melchisedech. All those remote people in the Old Testament are dragged in here, because we want to remind ourselves that the instinct of offering God sacrifice is an instinct which the human race had long before the Christian dispensation came to explain how the thing could be done. All those old sacrifices of bullocks and goats and rams under the Jewish Law, and, in their way, even the sacrifices offered by the old pagans to their gods when they were trying to do their best, are caught up and contained (that is the point, I think) in this supreme sacrifice which our Lord's Death has now made it possible for us to offer. I expect when you were about six or seven you probably knitted a pair of garters for your father as a birthday present, which were quite hopeless as garters because they wouldn't even meet at the back, or produced some equally inconvenient and embarrassing gift, for which he had to express the most energetic gratitude. Well, suppose on his next birthday you produce a present which is really worth having; a pipe or a hot-water bottle or an umbrella or one of those things you simply can't get nowadays. Possibly as you give it him, you may say, " Remember those garters I gave you when I was a kid? " And his eye will light up with an indulgent smile, thinking of those garters. That's what we do, I think, when we say this prayer; we remind Almighty God of the poor, fumbling attempts we human creatures used to make at sacrifice before we knew any better; we go back to the childhood of our race, and remind ourselves and him that anyhow we meant well.

Then comes a curious piece; one is always coming across curious bits and pieces in the Mass. The priest bends down, and asks God that this sacrifice of ours may be carried by his holy Angel up to his altar in Heaven, there in the very presence of his Divine Majesty. We, he adds, are sharing the privileges of God's earthly altar here; and with that he bends down and kisses it—he can't help himself; it is so splendid having an altar on earth at all. We are going to do that by receiving the Body and Blood of his Son; and with that he makes the sign of the Cross over the Host and then over the Chalice, as if he wasn't quite certain that they had been blessed enough. And by doing that, he says, we hope to be filled up quite full with benediction and grace; and with that he makes the sign of the Cross over himself, as if to attract back to himself the blessing he has just given.

I say that's a curious bit, because after all why should it be necessary to have Angels carrying this sacrifice of ours up into Heaven? Surely it's there already. What lies before the priest is the Body of Christ, his natural Body which is also in Heaven. The whole thing, of course, is utterly beyond our comprehension, but let me give you a very crude illustration to explain what I mean. You know how you can get hold of a bit of looking-glass, or even a table-knife if you have very bad table-manners, and hold it so that it will catch the sunlight, and make it flash into the face of the girl opposite you? A thing I hope you never do. Well, there is one face you couldn't flash it into, however much you tried, and that is the face of the sun. Impossible that this bit of the sun's light should go up into the sky and be more part of the sun's light than it is. But aren't we asking the same sort of thing when we ask that the Body of our Lord Jesus Christ should be carried up to Heaven?

Well, the clever people say—and I fancy the clever people may be right—that this particular bit of the Mass doesn't really belong here; it has got here by accident. Probably it used to come earlier on, and perhaps at the Offertory. You may or may not remember that when I was talking about the *Suscipe, sancte Pater*, the prayer which comes right at the beginning of the Offertory, I pointed out how curiously it was phrased. It talked about the wafer on the paten as " this immaculate host ", as if it had already been consecrated. And I said, that doesn't matter because the Mass is all one action; there's no time in it really, there's no before and after in it really. Well, here we come up against the same point again. The priest refers to the unconsecrated host as if it were a consecrated Host, or he refers to the consecrated Host as if it were still an unconsecrated host, and it doesn't matter in one case or the other. In the Mass, we have pushed ourselves forward into eternity, and questions of time don't bother us.

That's all rather boring. But now we come on to one of the really delightful things about the Mass, though I'm never quite sure why it should be so delightful; I mean the Memento of the Dead. It always makes me rather want to cry. And perhaps the pathetic thing about it is that when we ask God to remember our dead it makes us remember how little *we* remember our dead. The clever people ask, Why is it *Memento etiam*, " Remember also "? There's no " also " about it; we haven't been reminding God of anything just before. I think if I knew one of the clever people I would point out what doesn't seem to have occurred to any of them—that the word *etiam* in Latin doesn't necessarily mean " also ". It can mean, " even now ". Don't you think that makes the prayer rather jollier? " Remember So-and-so, O Lord, even now; even now, although he's been dead such a long time; and we, who felt when he died as if nothing could ever make us forget, hardly ever think about him. Other people, other interests have come into our lives; and only now and again some anniversary, or a scene recalling the past, brings back to us, faint and remote, the memory that was once so fresh and so poignant. But you, Lord, are not like that; you are eternal, and you remember the dead even now, just as if they had only died yesterday." I think that justifies the *etiam* all right.

But you're young, and please God you haven't known yet what it was to lose somebody you loved; or if so you haven't yet known the treacherous feeling of having forgotten them. Let me give you another reason why, from the priest's point of view at any rate, I think this memento of the dead is rather splendid. He looks down at the sacred Host, and sees in it a window between this world and the supernatural world. Of course when I say that you think it is rather irreverent; one shouldn't talk about the sacred Body of our Blessed Lord as a window. But, you know, you oughtn't to be always trying to catch me out in being heretical like that; there's more to be said for my point of view than you think. The APPEARANCES of bread and wine are still there, really there, and they belong to earth. That is one side of the window, if you see what I mean, and the other side of the window is the SUBSTANCE which underlies them; our Lord's Body and Blood, which are in Heaven. So, at Benediction, and at this point in the Mass, I like to think of myself as standing outside a window; not being able to see, alas, what is going on inside, but comforted by the thought that there is an inside. Let me put it like this.

You are passing along the street, and you see a light in one particular window; and you know that that room belongs to a great friend of yours. The blind is down, perhaps, or at any rate you can't see anything interesting from the level of the street. But it gives you a nice cosy feeling to reflect that your friend

IS in there, and to imagine her sitting and reading a book, with the wireless on, or scratching the dog's ears. Very likely she isn't in there really; I expect most of your friends leave the light on. But it's good to have the feeling that there's only a sheet of glass between her and you. When we pray for the Holy Souls, we may be quite wrong; the person you are praying for may be in Heaven really. But it's nice to think that our prayers are helping them—and if they aren't, you may be very sure they are helping somebody else—to grow out of Purgatory upwards and onwards into light and peace. You on one side of the window, and your friend on the other; we on one side of the sacred Host, seeing the appearances, our dead on the other, almost within reach, now, of grasping the substance.

Once more, notice, although the priest is allowed to think of particular people, and you are meant to think of particular people at this point, the prayer of the Church adds, " To them, Lord, and to ALL who lie asleep in Christ ". The Church never allows us to be selfish in our prayers; she always makes us think of the other people we didn't know, whose death was a grief, whose memory is a sacred thing, to other people, not us. At the end of the prayer the priest bows his head; some say, because our Lord bowed his in dying.

And then, just when you are feeling all nice and cosy about the faithful departed, an interruption comes. The priest, who has been quite silent up till now ever since the *Sanctus*, suddenly beats his breast and says in a rather loud voice: " To us also, to us sinners." The point is, I think, that it is time we stopped day-dreaming, and thinking about the past, as we often do when the dead come into our minds. Purgatory is only an interlude; the thing which matters is somehow to get people out of this world into Heaven. So, rousing us with his raised voice, he goes on to pray that we may have some kind of part and lot with God's holy apostles and martyrs. And then he goes off into a long supplementary list of saints' names, which he left out in the first part of the Canon. One very important omission he now makes good—except for our Blessed Lady, that earlier list only included the names of *men* saints. Now we come in for Perpetua and Agatha and Lucy and Agnes and Cecilia and Anastasia; and St. Agnes, we remember with some interest, was only twelve or thirteen years old when she was martyred; so there is some point in asking that we may have part and lot with *her*.

Well, then there are more headaches for the clever people; why does the priest wind up this prayer by telling God that it is through Jesus Christ he hallows and vitalizes and blesses *all* these good things? Surely he ought only to be thinking of what lies on the corporal and what is contained in the Chalice; why *all* these good things? Well, I dare say I'm quite wrong here, but I'm inclined to think that at this culminating point in the sacrifice, just when he is getting on to the *Pater noster* with its prayer for our daily bread, the priest remembers how the offerings we made, bread and wine, were things to which God gave his blessing in the natural as well as in the supernatural order; they were only specimens of all those good gifts which God showers on us. This is our Eucharist, our thanksgiving, and we are going to praise God not only for the graces he has given us through the

Redemption, but for all the blessings we have, sun and new flowers and the fire on the hearth and poetry and friendship and everything that lights up life for us; they are all his gifts, and in offering up the best of all his gifts we want to remember all of them. Through him who redeemed the world, the world itself, with all its light and colour, was made. Through him and together with him and in him we offer to the Father, that Father who is one with him through the bond of the Holy Spirit, all honour and all glory for ever and ever and ever.

XIII

PATER NOSTER TO ITE MISSA EST

And they went back, each to his own home. John vii.

XIII

PATER NOSTER TO ITE MISSA EST

And they went back, each to his own home.
John vii.

Now we get on to the *Pater noster*.

You will remember that our Lord, in the sermon on the mount, warned his disciples not to use vain repetitions when they were at their prayers. And by way of teaching them not to use vain repetitions, he taught them the *Pater noster*. The result of which is that we find ourselves saying the *Pater noster* about two dozen times a day, and rather wonder sometimes what vain repetition means, if it doesn't mean this sort of thing. Well, actually, I don't think that is what the Greek word means, and so in my version I have translated it, " Do not use many phrases "; I think it's a warning against saying complicated sort of prayers and expecting them to be effective because they are complicated, which is what the heathen did. But I suppose it remains true that most of us do find these constantly repeated prayers, the Our Father and the Hail Mary especially, become so familiar that it's almost impossible to remember what they mean while we are reciting them; they slip off our tongues by force of habit, and we don't really *mean* " thy kingdom come " when we say the *Pater noster*, any more than we feel any interest in the state of health enjoyed by the lady who has come to tea when we say " How do you do? " to her.

I expect this is very cowardly advice; but for myself I always think it's not much use trying to fight against this particular kind of distraction, trying to make ourselves *feel* every single petition in the Our Father every time we say it. No, I think it's meant to be a sort of taking-off-from-the-ground when we want to set free the wings of prayer. And therefore what I would recommend is getting hold of just one idea in a prayer like that, either the first idea that comes along, or the idea that appeals to us most, or the idea that appeals to us most at this particular moment, and hanging on to that all through our recitation of the prayer itself; the words OUR FATHER, for example, are quite enough by themselves to key one up, don't you think? I don't see why we shouldn't just bask in that idea, sun ourselves in that idea, of God's fatherhood, and let the rest of the prayer slip past us while we are about it. But with this recitation of the *Pater noster* at Mass, I'm afraid it's worse than that so far as I am concerned; I don't think I try to concentrate on any single phrase in it, I just babble it out with a delightful sense that I am TALKING TO GOD. With most of our prayers, I mean, we feel—at least I do—as if we were talking into a microphone, knowing that as a matter of fact there is Somebody listening, but not having the sense, the awareness, that our mind is in direct contact with another Mind. But the *Pater noster* at Mass is somehow like sitting over the fire with somebody else sitting over the fire in the opposite chimney-corner, talking about a hundred things, perhaps, important and unimportant, perhaps just sitting there and not bothering to say much, but with the sense, the awareness, of somebody else's presence. If you feel like that about the *Pater noster* at Mass—or about any other bit of the prayers you say in the course of the day—don't bother to disturb your intimacy with God by deliberately and laboriously *thinking* about this or that; just stop thinking and throw yourself into the experience of being with him.

So I'm not going to tell you what you ought to be thinking about during the *Pater noster*, because as I say I have a strong suspicion that one is best occupied in not thinking about anything. We will go on to the prayer which follows, the *Libera nos*. At the end of the *Pater noster*, you see, there is a bit of dialogue. The priest stops short after *Et ne nos inducas in tentationem*, the server is supposed to say *Sed libera nos a malo*. And the priest picks up that idea, as it were, and turns it over in his mind. "Deliver us from evil? Do you know, I think that's a good idea of yours." What a lot of evils you and I want to be delivered from, when you come to think of it! From past evils; that is, from sins committed long ago, which have been remitted, please God, but still have left their mark on us, left us with a debt to be paid, and bad habits to fight against. And present evils, the ones we are thinking about just now, and said we would remember in the Mass; that fountain-pen that was lost nearly a fortnight ago, and our aunt's pleurisy. And future evils, the ones we aren't thinking about just now, and aren't going to think about just now, because our Lord doesn't like us to fret about the morrow; but there are all sorts of unpleasant things that might happen to us and our friends and our country and the world at large; we won't think about them, but we do want to be delivered from them. Let's leave it to the saints. . . . That's one advantage, I always think, about invoking the blessed saints; they *know*. They see the world all mapped out from above like a photograph taken from an aeroplane; we only see what's in front of our noses. So it's a good thing to say, Dear St. Anthony, you know what is the grace I most need; will you please ask for that? Dear St. Anthony, you know which is the next crisis that the world is going to be up against; please stave it off. (Rather like the mother who told her daughter to go upstairs and see what Johnny was doing and tell him not to.) So we fall back on the saints again; our Lady of course, and St. Peter and St. Paul, and then the apostles, St. Andrew and . . . what's that? Oh, got to get on with the Mass, have we? All right, St. Andrew and all the other saints. That, I suppose, is why St. Andrew always get his mention here; the only place in the liturgy where he is singled out like that; I'm glad, aren't you? Because he does deserve some reward for being the first saint who heard our Lord's call and said, " All right, Lord; coming ".

At the word " Andrew ", the priest takes the paten out from under the corporal, where (I forgot to tell you) it has been hidden ever since the Offertory, and crosses himself with it, and slips it under the Sacred Host. Then he takes the Sacred Host itself, holds it over the Chalice, breaks it in two, puts down the right-hand half, and holds the left-hand half over the Chalice again while he detaches quite a little fragment from it; then puts down the left-hand half, but still holds the little fragment over the Chalice while he says *Per omnia saecula saeculorum*. The server, who is beginning to get into the swing of the thing, pipes up AMEN. And the priest says, " The peace of the Lord be always with you ". There is a lot of peace going about at this point in the Mass. You know how all the people in choir at High Mass start giving one another stage kisses soon afterwards. And if you do the proper thing and marry a Catholic and have a nuptial Mass, it is at this point that you and he go right up to the altar step and have a special blessing given you, which is very consoling and a great argument against mixed marriages.

What is it all about? Immediately after he has said " The peace of the Lord be always with you " the priest lets the little fragment fall into the Chalice, so that it remains in, and as it were becomes part of, the Precious Blood. Now, I don't know what is the true explanation of all that. But the mystical account they give of it is rather nice. They say that the breaking of the Host in two represents the breaking of our Lord's Body on the Cross, represents therefore his Passion, and the re-uniting of the two sacred Species when the fragment is dropped into the Chalice represents the Resurrection, our Lord's Soul returning to his Body. And that gives you something to think about while the fraction is being made. Because what is meant to happen to us Christian people, so that we shall be like our Lord, is that we should be broken. Our wills must somehow be broken, usually by a painful process; having to do uncongenial work, being misunderstood by other people, being let down by other people, losing those we love by death, being torn away from familiar ties and affections we thought we couldn't do without—somehow our Lord has got to break our wills and make us give in to him. Then comes peace; it isn't till our wills are broken to him that we begin to understand real peace. And then comes resurrection, the mending up again of the broken thing, so that we are infinitely stronger than ever. But I don't expect you'll understand about all that just yet.

What follows that is the *Agnus Dei*. Notice that we have been talking to the First Person of the Blessed Trinity all through the Mass so far, and referring to our Lord as if he wasn't in the room. Now, till the Communion is over, we talk to our Lord and to him only. We appeal to him, the Victim loaded with a world's guilt, for pardon, and then for pardon again and then for peace. We say three prayers, one asking him to unite Christendom, one asking that we may never be separated from him, one asking that when he comes to us in Communion he may find us in right dispositions, and may increase the health of our souls. I say, find us in right dispositions; not find us worthy to receive him—we are never that. Never talk about receiving Communion worthily; it's a misleading phrase. *Domine, non sum dignus, Domine, non sum dignus, Domine, non sum dignus;* Lord, you must force your way in, not take any notice of my soul's untidiness; it's not the least bit ready for you really.

Of the Communion itself, there's no need to speak.

Nor do I want to talk about the verse taken from scripture marked Communion, or the prayer marked Post-Communion; We must hurry on to the big moment when the priest turns round and says *Ite missa est*.

You can tell it is a big moment, because at High Mass the deacon sings it to a very long and elaborate chant which goes up and down all over the place. When I first went on as deacon, at St. Edmund's, I went out into the drive after breakfast to have a last rehearsal all by myself, and the moment I started I—i—i . . . every single rook in every tree in the drive got up and left, so I felt like St. Francis preaching to the birds. Why is it necessary to tell the people to go away? They are beginning to think about breakfast anyhow. Why is it necessary to tell them that " our massing is over ", or whatever that odd phrase *Ite missa est* means? Why, I think the point is what I tried to suggest in the introductory sermon: " they went back, each to his own home." Hitherto, we have been a crowd, we Mass-goers, trying to remember our solidarity in Christ. But Communion means the coming of Christ to the individual soul, and that breaks the charm; the priest wants to be alone to make his thanksgiving; each of you wants to be alone to make hers. So the *Ite missa est* is the signal for the breaking-up of a party.

I'm afraid that is what this sermon is, so far as I am concerned. I shall be away next Sunday, so this is the last chance I shall have of saying Thank you. Thank you, I mean, for wanting to have sermons preached to you, and for taking some interest in what the sermon was about. But, of course, the real bond between us, these last six or seven years, is not that I've been preaching sermons to you, good, bad or indifferent, but that you and I have been breaking bread together; sharing, day after day and week after week, that food whose giving and taking ought to be unforgettable, because its effects are eternal. Goodness knows how many times you've watched me turn round and greet you with the *Dominus vobiscum*, or pass from side to side of the sanctuary asking God to keep *this* and *this* and *this* soul safe till it reaches eternal life. When you have left Aldenham, there will be plenty of things to remind me of you; I shall find myself still walking warily through the passages for fear of cannoning into somebody, still keeping my window shut in case one of you should come along and exchange a few words with a friend in the dormitory upstairs; an inkstain here, a thumb-mark there, will recall the memory of your visit. But you won't find it so easy to remember me; you will grow into your new surroundings very soon, and they will be different surroundings. Only one thing is never different; the Holy Mass. Every now and then, perhaps, some gesture, some trick of manner about the priest who serves your chapel there will bring back to you memories of Aldenham; you will find yourself saying, " Do you remember how old What's-his-name always used to blow his nose during the server's Confiteor? " And that will be something, if it helps to remind you that What's-his-name exists, or anyhow existed. I will leave you with the request which St. Monica made, just before she died, of her son St. Augustine: " I only ask you to remember me at the altar of the Lord."

Destiny is always jumbling up the pattern of our lives like the patterns in a kaleidoscope. You can't avoid it, even by entering holy religion; you take a vow of stability, only to find that life is one long round of packing. The charmed circle is always being broken up; we are separated from the people we have grown accustomed to. But do let's get it clearly in our heads that there can be no real separation, in life or in death, as long as we stick to the Holy Mass. In Christ we are all one; the sacred Host is the focus in which all our rays meet, regardless of time and space. Only we must keep true to him; only we must all go on saying that prayer the priest says before his Communion, asking that though he is separated from everything else he may never be separated from our Blessed Lord; *A te numquam, a te numquam, a te numquam separari permittas.*